EDGAR CAYCE

ON THE DEAD SEA SCROLLS

BY GLENN D. KITTLER
UNDER THE EDITORSHIP OF
HUGH LYNN CAYCE
Director, Association for Research and Enlightenment

WARNER BOOKS

A Warner Communications Company

WARNER BOOKS EDITION

Cover design by Karen Katz

Warner Books, Inc.
666 Fifth Avenue
New York, N.Y. 10103

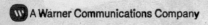 A Warner Communications Company

Printed in the United States of America

First Printing: December, 1970

Reissued: June, 1988

10

**Was Christianity born in Bethlehem—
or was it conceived a century before
the birth of Christ along the
rocky, desolate shores of the Dead Sea?**

▶ ◀

For more than 40 years, Edgar Cayce served as a powerful spiritual channeler, transmitting more than 14,000 mystical messages between the metaphysical and material planes. Yet the astounding revelations surrounding the discovery of the Dead Sea Scrolls —and the mysterious religious sect known as the Essenes—perplexed and disturbed even the psychic himself.

- Was Mary—the mother of Christ—only one of eleven other virgins chosen to serve as possible physical channels for the coming Messiah?
- Could she—like Jesus—have been "immaculately conceived" in fulfillment of her destiny, then go on to bear Joseph two "natural" children—siblings of Christ?
- Was it possible that the path of spiritual enlightenment took Jesus first to Persia then to India, where he studied healing, meditation, and astrology?
- And perhaps most startling of all: Were Mary, Joseph, John the Baptist, the innkeeper at Bethlehem, and Christ himself all members of the spiritually evolved monastic tribe known as the Essenes?

In this eye-opening book, Glenn D. Kittler draws upon hundreds of Cayce's most powerful prophecies to reveal the secrets of the Essenes: a mysterious sect whose mystical powers forged a religious movement— and whose story will forever alter your perception of true spiritual enlightenment.

Author's Note: For the sake of clarity and pertinence, several of the extracts from the Edgar Cayce Life Readings quoted in this book have been edited slightly and thus are not verbatim.

INTRODUCTION

EDGAR CAYCE ON THE DEAD SEA SCROLLS

The discovery in 1947 of an Essene community (according to most of the scholars who examined it) on the northwest coast of the Dead Sea seemed to have been an archaeological confirmation of Edgar Cayce's psychic readings given over a period of more than eleven years prior to that time. Retrocognitive psychic capacity seems to have been exercised in more than twenty-five-hundred psychic readings by Edgar Cayce. Nowhere is it more exciting than in the descriptions of the abandoned community now known as Qumran.

This community is closely identified as the place where the famous Dead Sea Scrolls were written, copied and finally hidden in the caves around the Dead Sea.

Qumran would not be so significant as a focus of psychic information were it not for the fact that it has been well established that the community was in operation for at least a hundred years prior to the birth of Jesus and for sixty-eight years after his death. Situated as it is in the geographic center of locations of highly significant events in His life, such as the baptism by John the Baptist, just a few miles away; the forty days in the wilderness, not far from an easy route from Jerusalem to Jericho; the community has been the subject of much theological and scholarly debate as to how much Jesus knew about this place, the inhabitants and their work on the scrolls.

The Edgar Cayce readings suggest, as you will see, close connections between many of Jesus' intimate associates (Zebedee, John, James, Andrew, John the Baptist, etc.) and the community. One cannot help wondering, since Edgar Cayce was correct about the location of the community eleven years prior to its discovery, could he also be right about Jesus' early associations with the Essenes?

It seems to me fortunate that a skillful, unprejudiced writer has been secured to tell the story in a carefully balanced and readable style. Glenn D. Kittler has a Catholic background, including a considerable religious interest in New Testament times. He has only a general, open-minded interest in ESP, and so does not press for acceptance of the Edgar Cayce data. It seems to me that this is an excellent subject for such objectivity.

For some of you, this may be the first introduction to Edgar Cayce. "Who was he?"

It depends on through whose eyes you look at him. A goodly number of his contemporaries knew the "waking" Edgar Cayce as a gifted professional photographer. Another group (predominantly children) admired him as a warm and friendly Sunday School teacher. His own family knew him as a wonderful husband and father.

The "sleeping" Edgar Cayce was an entirely different figure—a psychic known to thousands of people, in all walks of life, who had cause to be grateful for his help. Indeed, many of them believed that he alone had either saved or changed their lives when all seemed lost. The "sleeping" Edgar Cayce was a medical diagnostician, a prophet, and a devoted proponent of Bible lore.

Even as a child, on a farm near Hopkinsville, Kentucky, where he was born on March 18, 1877, Edgar Cayce displayed powers of perception which seemed to extend beyond the normal range of the five senses. At the age of six or seven he told his parents that he was able to see and talk to "visions," sometimes of relatives who had recently died. His parents attributed this to the overactive imagination of a lonely child who had been influenced by the dramatic language of the revival meetings which were popular in that section of the country. Later, by sleeping with his head on his schoolbooks, he developed some form of photographic memory which helped him advance rapidly in the country school. This gift faded, however, and Edgar was only able to complete his seventh grade before he had to seek his own place in the world.

By the age of twenty-one, he had become the salesman for a wholesale stationery company. At this time he developed a gradual paralysis of the throat muscles, which threatened the loss of his voice. When doctors were unable to find a physical cause for this condition, hypnosis was tried, but failed to have any permanent effect. As a last resort, Edgar asked a friend to help him reenter the same kind of hypnotic sleep that had enabled him to memorize his schoolbooks as a child. His friend gave him the necessary suggestion, and once he was in a self-induced trance, Edgar came to grips with his own problem. He recommended medication and manipulative therapy which successfully restored his voice and repaired his system.

A group of physicians from Hopkinsville and Bowling Green, Kentucky, took advantage of his unique talent to diagnose their own patients. They soon discovered that Cayce only needed to be given the name and address of a patient, wherever he was, to be able to tune in telepathically on that individual's mind and body as easily as if they were both in the same room. He needed, and was given, no other information regarding any patient.

One of the young M.D.'s, Dr. Wesley Ketchum, submitted a report on this unorthodox procedure to a clinical research society in Boston. On October 9, 1910, *The New York Times* carried two pages of headlines and pictures. From that day on, troubled people from all over the country sought help from the "wonder man."

When Edgar Cayce died on January 3, 1945, in Virginia Beach, Virginia, he left well over 14,000 documented stenographic records of the telepathic-clairvoyant statements he had given for more than six thousand different people over a period of forty-three years. These documents are referred to as "readings."

The readings constitute one of the largest and most impressive records of psychic perception ever to emanate from a single individual. Together with their relevant records, correspondence and reports, they have been cross-indexed under thousands of subject headings and placed at the disposal of psychologists, students, writers

9

and investigators who still come, in increasing numbers, to examine them.

A foundation known as the A.R.E. (Association for Research and Enlightenment, Inc., P. O. Box 595, Virginia Beach, Virginia 23451) was founded in 1932 to preserve these readings. As an open-membership research society, it continues to index and catalog the information, initiate investigation and experiments, and promote conferences, seminars and lectures. Until now, its published findings have been made available only to its members through its own publishing facilities.

—*Hugh Lynn Cayce*

ONE

The summer afternoon was stifling hot, but a good breeze came in from the sea, cooling the house. In a downstairs room at the back of the house, a man lay on a couch. His collar was opened, his shoelaces were untied, his belt was loose. He appeared to be asleep, and yet he was talking. His wife was there. His older son was there. Nearby sat a woman writing in shorthand all that the man was saying. And nearby sat another woman, still young at sixty-two, gray, but with a smooth, unlined face still pretty, and with bright blue eyes that now intently studied the man on the couch. She leaned forward, listening, for she knew he was talking about her.

"We find the entity," he said, meaning this woman, "was in that land of the Nativity, when the Master walked the earth, when there were those who gathered to listen, to interpret—to seek not only physical but mental and spiritual relief and understanding. The entity then was among those of the holy women and those in close acquaintance-ship with many who were the teachers or the apostles or the disciples—many of those women, as Mary, Martha, Elizabeth. All of these were as friends—yea, companions

10

of the entity during the experience. For the entity then was in that capacity as one of the holy women who ministered in the temple service and in the preparation of those who dedicated their lives for individual activity during the sojurn. The entity was then what would be termed in the present, in some organizations, a Sister Superior or an officer, as it were, in those of the Essenes and their preparations.

"Hence we find the entity then giving, giving, ministering, encouraging, making for the greater activities, and making for those encouraging experiences oft in the lives of the Disciples, coming in contact with the Master oft in the ways between Bethany, Galilee, Jerusalem. For, as indicated, the entity kept the school on the way above Emmaus to the way that goeth down towards Jericho and towards the northernmost coast from Jerusalem.

"The name then was Eloise; and the entity blessed many of those who came to seek to know the teachings, the ways, the mysteries, the understandings. For the entity had been trained in the schools of those that were of the prophets and prophetesses; and the entity was indeed a prophetess in those experiences, and thus gained throughout."

These words were spoken on the afternoon of June 22, 1937, in a house on Arctic Crescent in Virginia Beach, Virginia. The man on the couch was Edgar Cayce. When he finished speaking, he took several deep breaths, and then he sat up, refreshed and feeling a little hungry. He looked at the woman who had been taking shorthand notes and he asked: "Gladys, what did I say?"

He had said this: This other woman—the entity—had lived before, and more than once. In the days when Jesus Christ was a young man in Palestine, this woman lived there and she knew Him. She held a position of authority in a school—a house of studies, actually—of the Essene community. It was located along the road east from Emmaus to the Dead Sea, where it turned north to Jericho. As Eloise, she had known Mary, the mother of Jesus; she knew Mary's cousin Elizabeth, the mother of John the Baptist; she knew Martha of Bethany, sister of Lazarus who was raised from the dead. She knew the Apostles and the Disciples. She had been trained in the

11

schools of the prophets, and this, of necessity, meant that she had lived for a while at least on Mount Carmel where the Prophet Elijah and his monks had lived in caves almost a thousand years before. The sojourn—the life experience—had been a good one. By choosing to serve as an Essene and to assist Jesus Christ in the preparation for His messianic purpose, the entity had moved its soul closer to God.

The date again: June 22, 1937.

In the Edgar Cayce archives, the entity is, for the sake of her own privacy and the privacy of those who were her relatives in the present sojourn, listed as Life Reading 1391. She has since died again, perhaps for the last time.

On April 25, 1948, *The New York Times* printed on Page 6 a short and somewhat vague but fascinating article. Certain ancient documents had been found in the Holy Land and some of them had reached the United States. They were very old, perhaps pre-Christian, perhaps of Biblical significance. They had been found in a cave on the western shore of the Dead Sea, but no one was sure when. Scholars were now appraising the documents.

These documents became known as the Dead Sea Scrolls, and they created a storm among the world's scholars. They were identified as the work of Essenes, a Jewish sect which seemed to have disappeared without a trace sometime during the first century of Christianity. So little was known about them that the sudden discovery of documents attributable to them served only to deepen the mystery and spark controversy.

Why should the documents be there in an inaccessible mountain cave in the heart of a wasteland?

About a mile to the south, on the marly plateau called Wadi Qumran, were some ruins. Archaeologists had known about them for a long time and took them to be the remains of a Roman fort. So many forts had been excavated that another one held no special attraction, so this one was ignored. But the discovery of the Dead Sea Scrolls changed this attitude. Besides the documents mentioned in the *Times,* additional scrolls were being found in other caves along the sea, until they became so numerous that there was no other explanation for them than the likelihood that they had been written in the vicinity and hidden at some moment of danger.

Digging at the Qumran ruins began in the summer of 1949 and continued for five years. What was uncovered was not a Roman fort at all. It was identified as an Essene establishment. A monastery. A house of studies. A school.

And it was right where Edgar Cayce said it was, a dozen years before.

The only source from which Edgar Cayce might have learned about the Essene monastery before he mentioned it during a reading in 1937 was from a book called *Historica Naturalis,* written by Pliny the Elder around 70 A. D. A naturalist who wrote down his observations while traveling on duty with the Roman army, Pliny did comment that while in Judea he came upon an Essene monastery on the western shores of the Dead Sea, just north of Engedi, and it was probably the same place. But there is little likelihood that Edgar Cayce ever heard of Pliny, less likelihood that he ever read the book. Though Edgar Cayce was devoted to the Bible and read it daily for almost sixty years, the Essenes are not even mentioned in it. What is more likely, according to those who knew Edgar Cayce best, is that he never gave the Essenes a thought until he began to do Life Readings and would awaken and be told that he had · spoken about them while in the trance.

In trance ("while asleep" would be more accurate), Cayce often spoke of the Essenes, even before 1937. One aspect of his comments was in contradiction to the view generally held by scholars. Scholars have traditionally believed that the Essenes, if they existed at all, were cloistered, celibate monks. They supposedly recruited new members either by accepting mature men who wanted to get away from the world or taking in the sons of outside families, provided that the boys were young enough not to be already too influenced by the ways of the world. However, some early writers have indicated that sexual intercourse was permissible for lower-ranking monks but only for the purpose of begetting male infants

13

who would then be raised in the monastery. Women, then, played little, if any, roles in the Essene milieu.

During numerous Life Readings, Edgar Cayce, on the other hand, told women besides Entity 1391 that they had been active in Essene communities, playing vital, even critical, roles not only in the Essene milieu but in the actual birth, training and public ministry of Jesus Christ. According to the readings, only a fraction of the Essenes lived for any length of time in what can be described as a monastery. Thousands of them resided throughout the Middle East, all of them leading what would be considered normal lives for the Jews of their time, and all of them bound together by the conviction that the Messiah would become man through their ranks.

Evidence supporting a significant factor of the readings came to light during the excavations at Qumran. At this point, the beach, if it can be called that, is about a mile wide, ending abruptly at the promontory in which are the caves where the scrolls were found. The monastery is inland, almost at the promontory, and between the monastery and the sea a large cemetery has been uncovered. Experts have said that some of the skeletons have been identified as those of women, even girls. In this regard, therefore, the readings appear more accurate than tradition.

Even so, the credibility of the Edgar Cayce readings is not at issue. In fact, the content of many of the readings were quite incredible to Cayce himself. He had been a devout Presbyterian. For years he taught Sunday School, until the growing demands for his psychic counseling deprived him of the time and energy. He was, on all counts, an orthodox Christian. Some of his utterances while asleep were certainly unorthodox—and he knew it when he had them read back to him. However, these utterances had not come *from* him but *through* him. He was, in a sense, being used. He hoped it was by God, but he could not explain why.

Describing his own role during a psychical experience, Edgar Cayce said that the last event of which he was consciously aware was a blinding flash of light. He then found himself in a vast room, its walls lined with large volumes—the Hall of Records. Someone was there—the

Keeper of the Records, but Cayce never described him. Whoever was conducting the reading—usually Cayce's wife Gertrude or his older son Hugh Lynn—would then put to him the matter to be discussed. The Keeper of the Records would indicate a certain volume. Without actually touching it or actually reading it, Cayce seemed to know its contents, and he would begin to speak. After an initial statement, he would answer questions. Readings usually lasted about a half-hour. When Cayce awoke, he had no idea of what he had said and was often as astounded by his own words as those who had heard them.

Edgar Cayce put such trust in the probability that his psychic faculties were a gift from God that he was extremely sensitive about his use of them. He felt it was wrong to use the faculties to determine some means for materialistic acquisitions. An incident occurred in 1944 that demonstrated this conviction in a touching way. Among the many people making inquiries of Cayce was a New Hampshire woman who held a doctorate in education and also did some writing. She wasn't having much luck with her writing. Since it was not necessary for án entity to be in Cayce's presence for a reading, this woman, as did most others, consulted him by mail. One day she sent him a list of twenty-five questions, about half of which dealt with her writing. She wanted Cayce to give her the names of some publishers who, according to his psychical insight, would accept her writings. She had other questions about her job as a professor, others about some family problems, others about travel plans. Cayce wrote back to her:

"I, of course, don't like to question anyone's approach to information of this kind, but it seems to me, Doctor, there are many questions in your list here that could be answered through other sources rather than undertaking to get it through a source of this kind. And the questions are so scattered! Can't you have them all one subject, in a more uniform manner? This is not fortune-telling, Doctor; it is a universal consciousness, if it is anything at all. See if you can't change these a little bit. I think you could get much more out of it."

All that Edgar Cayce hoped people would get out of

15

his readings was a guidepost to a better spiritual life. For a while, he thought of entering the ministry as his means of leading people to God, but events of his life precluded this. Though Cayce had been aware of his psychic faculties since boyhood, he was in his forties before he realized that these same faculties could open the past to him, and open the future as well. His readings in both directions inescapably moved him into the area of theology. But he merely reported what he experienced. He did not preach. He did not seek to convert. If some of the things he reported struck others as blasphemous or heretical, so be it. For others, the Edgar Cayce readings fill great gaps in the life of the best known and the best loved man who ever lived—the Son of God.

The existence of the first Dead Sea Scrolls became known in the spring of 1947, but the exact date of the discovery is still uncertain. It may have been as much as a year before. The discovery was an accident.

Some Bedouins of the Ta'amire tribe were making their way from Jordan into Palestine. This was the period of the Arab-Jewish war which, in 1948, brought about the partitioning of Palestine and created the state of Israel. At the time, there were check points at bridges on the River Jordan, then the border between Palestine and Jordan, where travelers could cross from one country to the other after having their identification papers approved. The Bedouins avoided these places. They were carrying a cargo of contraband which they intended to sell to Arabs at Bethlehem. Thus they stayed on the byways of Jordan until they reached a lonely stretch along the river where they knew they could cross into Palestine undetected.

In Palestine, they continued southward to the Dead Sea and proceeded south along its western shore. The only place in the area where they could get fresh water was at the springs at 'Ain Feshkha, less than a mile south of Wadi Qumran. Wadi is an Arab word meaning a dry ravine that becomes a waterway during the rainy season. Wadi Qumran is a deep, rugged, severe ravine which ends so abruptly at the sea that during the rainy season it becomes a waterfall. Bible experts believe that about eight hundred years before Christ a small settlement existed here, called the City of Salt, just as the Dead Sea was then called the Sea of Salt. For centuries, the area has been desolate and deserted.

The site was, therefore, a safe rendezvous where the smugglers could await others of their tribe who were en route from Jordan. One day a boy—Muhammed The Wolf, by name—was assigned to tend the goats. He followed them northward, to the Wadi Qumran and beyond a half-mile. He noticed a cave on the bluffs, and to amuse himself, he started throwing stones at it, hoping for a bull's-eye. Finally one stone arched perfectly and disappeared into the cave. The boy was startled to hear the sound of breakage come from the cave. Quickly he drove the goats back to the camp, and told a friend of his what had happened. The two boys went back to the cave.

For years, Bedouins have known that the Holy Land abounds in objects of value to scientists whose purpose is to unearth the past. For over a century, archaeologists have been digging up the region, trying to find the missing links of history that lie below the surface of this formidable land, beneath its waters, in its caves. These valuable objects, whether they are bones, artifacts, weapons, writings, domiciles, serve to fill in the gaps of history between what is known and what is legend, and their value increases with their age and the legends they substantiate. Archaeological expeditions have been carried out on every continent, but those in the Holy Land have been of particular importance because of their religious significance. The Bible is a history book as well as a book on faith and morals; and when scientists can dig up evidence that a certain Biblical event did indeed occur where and when the Bible says it did, then the history book serves to confirm the book on faith and morals. Though millions of Christians believe that the Bible is Divinely inspired, scholars have found the book to be vague on certain points, contradictory on others, and have no comment on others mentioned in contemporary writings. Some of these criticisms may be the fault of men who have transcribed and translated the Bible through the centuries; some of the fault may belong to those who decided what should go into the Bible and what should stay out; some of the

17

fault may be the simple fact that the truths that can clear away the objections and overcome the criticisms are still there, deep in the soil, beneath the waters, in the caves, waiting to be discovered.

Scientists have made many important discoveries in the Holy Land, but many equally important discoveries have been made by the Bedouins. This place has been home to these nomad Semites since before Moses. They know it. Mostly illiterate, they are great storytellers, and legends generations old are still told each night around their campfires. Often these tales contain clues which are helpful to archaeologists in their search for antiquities. The clues are also helpful to the Bedouins, now that they have learned the value of the ancient items. By law, the antiquities belong to the government of the country where they are found—Palestine, previously, and now Israel and Jordan. When a university or a foundation pays for an archaeological expedition, it is usually possible to make arrangements with the government to borrow the findings for a while either to put them on public display elsewhere or to study them in properly equipped laboratories. Sometimes a government will sell what has been found. There is, however, a busy black market in the Holy Land for these treasures, as the Bedouins have discovered. It would be impossible to determine how many millions of dollars in Biblical antiquities have secretly found their way via the Bedouins to the black market and into private collections around the world. In all likelihood, then, when Muhammed The Wolf and his friend went back to the cave at Qumran, they were as hopeful of finding a treasure as they were in solving the mystery of the strange noise.

They entered a cave that was about twenty-five feet long, seven feet wide and nine feet high. They came upon a number of tall clay jars with bowl-like lids. Scattered throughout the cave were fragments of other jars that had been broken. Who broke them? Evidently Muhammed The Wolf had broken one with his good throw. Experts now believe that the others had probably been broken by earlier Bedouins who had been in the cave and broke the jars to find out what they contained.

The two boys removed the lids from some of the intact

18

jars and were repulsed by the bad odor that came from the inside. When they turned the jars upside down, cylindrical objects fell out, and they were wrapped in linen. The boys took a few of the objects down to the beach, where they removed the linen and beheld rolled up sheets of what seemed to be leather or parchment. They were able to unroll a couple of the sheets, and there was writing on them. The writing did not look like the Arabic script the boys had seen on shops and in newspapers when they were in towns, so they took their find back to the camp and showed the scrolls to their elders. The elders could not identify the writing; but since the scrolls had been found in a cave, as other valuables had before, they decided to take five of them into Bethlehem and try to sell them on the black market.

In Bethlehem, they offered the scrolls for the equivalent of sixty dollars to the merchant who bought the contraband they had brought from Jordan. The man didn't know what the scrolls were and wasn't interested. Next they went to the merchant from whom they always bought supplies for the trip back to Jordan. His name was Khalil Iskander Shahim; he was called Kando; he was a cobbler, and his shop was near the Church of the Nativity, which is believed to be on the site of the inn where Jesus Christ was born. Kando was a Syrian, and it seemed to him that the writing on the scrolls was ancient Syriac. He sent news of the scrolls by a Syrian friend to the Syrian Metropolitan (archbishop) at the Monastery of St. Mark in Old Jerusalem. The Metropolitan Mar Anthanasius Yeshue Samuel sent back word that he would like to examine the scrolls.

When one scroll was delivered to the Metropolitan, he broke off a sliver and burned it and decided it was leather. He recognized the writing as Hebrew, a language he could not read. What excited him, however, was learning where the scroll had been found. He knew that nobody had lived on the western shores of the Dead Sea since the First Century. If the scrolls were that old, they would be priceless. The Metropolitan informed Kando that he was ready to negotiate. This transaction had taken a few days, and the Bedouins, unwilling to stay in

19

Bethlehem too long with a war going on, had departed for Jordan, taking the other scrolls with them.

Months passed. Next time the Bedouins came from Jordan, they traveled by way of Jerusalem, then under martial law. They made contact with a Jewish merchant who inspected the scrolls and offered to buy them. He suggested that the Bedouins deliver the scrolls for payment next morning at his office in the New City. They agreed, then went on to Bethlehem for the night. They called on Kando and told him their good news, which was bad news for him. He warned them that, as Arabs, they might get arrested if they entered the Jewish-occupied New City without proper credentials. After this had the desired effect of frightening the Bedouins, Kando told them that he had a customer for the scrolls and that he could get a better price than the Jewish merchant had offered. Next day, he took the scrolls into the Old City and sold them to the Metropolitan for a reported one-hundred-fifty dollars. He gave the Arabs sixty dollars and told them to bring in any more scrolls they might find.

Oddly enough, months passed before Metropolitan Samuel definitely found out what a treasure he had acquired. The first thing he did was send two priests to Qumran to find out if the cave really was where the Bedouins had said it was. The priests found the cave, but they didn't find any unbroken jars. The reason: the Bedouins had already been back. They were using the jars for waterjugs and had given Kando additional scrolls. But the priests did find pieces of broken jars and fragments of scrolls.

The Metropolitan showed the scrolls to the experts who were available to him. This was in August, 1947, the hottest time of the year. Most of the foreign archaeologists were out of the country on vacation. Also, the war had made travel dangerous, thereby greatly decreasing the work that could be done and sending more experts away. There were Jewish experts in the country, of course, but most of them were in the fighting. Moreover, though Metropolitan Samuel was a Christian, he was also an Arab, and he did not want the Jewish scholars to have much to do with the scrolls until he knew more about them himself. At the moment, he knew very little.

The Jerusalem experts who examined the scrolls could not believe they were as old as the Metropolitan insisted they were. At most, the experts said, they might be two or three hundred years old, and one man suggested that they had been placed in the Qumran cave as recently as twenty-five years before. Hebrew law forbids the destruction of sacred books that have become too old for use. Each synagogue has a room, the genizah, where such books are allowed to age until they have deteriorated, and then they may be buried in the ground. It was suggested, therefore, that some Jewish community had recently put the scrolls in the cave to protect them from damage in the event of an Arab raid on their synagogue. In that event, the scrolls weren't worth much. The Metropolitan received the same discouragement when he took the scrolls to Syrian experts at Damascus. He had the same bad luck at Beirut.

Meanwhile, there was another development. Late in 1947, Professor E. L. Sukenik, chief archaeologist at the Hebrew University in the New City, returned from a trip abroad and heard rumors that somebody in Bethlehem had acquired some Hebrew writings that appeared to be of some age. This would be Kando. Through intermediaries, the two men made contact, and Professor Sukenik purchased two of the clay jars and four segments of scrolls. Before the year was out, he bought another scroll and some fragments. He was unable to date the material; but as he translated the scrolls and discovered they were of Biblical nature, he reached the genizah conclusion and said nothing about them.

Early in 1948, two American experts—Dr. William H. Brownless and Dr. John C. Trever—had a chance to examine the Metropolitan's scrolls, and they got excited. At last Metropolitan Samuel met somebody who was willing to concede that he might be right about the age of the scrolls. The Americans photographed the scrolls and sent the pictures to Professor William F. Albright of Johns Hopkins University, who notified them that the scrolls were indeed very old and that they surely were written before the time of Christ. A Jerusalem art dealer suggested that the Metropolitan put up his scrolls for sale on the European market. Instead, Metropolitan Samuel brought them to the United States himself. They were examined and confirmed at Yale and Johns Hopkins, and this was when *The New York Times* got wind of them.

In the New City, meantime, Professor Sukenik continued to study the scrolls and fragments he had. As 1948 unfolded, he acquired more fragments through Kando. Working with the professor was his son, also an archaeologist, and who was also famous as the military leader General Yigael Yadin. When they established to their satisfaction that their scrolls had been written in the First Christian Century and before, they made a public announcement to this effect at a press conference later in the year.

Surprisingly Metropolitan Samuel was unable to find an American buyer for his scrolls. Conflicting reasons for this have been put forth. There was, for example, some question of the legality of such a sale. On the partitioning of Palestine, the area where the scrolls had been found was given to Jordan, and when their existence became public knowledge, in 1949, the Jordanian government demanded their return. Actually there had been no legal government in Palestine at the time the Metropolitan acquired the scrolls, which was a point in his favor, and Arab experts to whom he had shown the scrolls had declared them worthless, which was another point. But there was the chance that Jordan might take the matter to the United Nations and perhaps win. Presumably nobody wanted to get involved in the wrangling.

Another reason given was another form of wrangling. Throughout 1949, *The New York Times* published numerous articles on the controversy which had developed among the experts on the dating of the scrolls, their historic validity and their religious significance. There was indication, in fact, that some religious leaders would have been happier if the scrolls had never been found at all. By then, little of the scroll writings had been published. Some of the scrolls had not even been unrolled. Leather scrolls turned to powder at the effort to open them. Two copper scrolls were so badly corroded that it seemed they would never be opened and read. Even so, from what scroll writings had been read, it began to appear that accepted Christian thought had not been originated by the first Christians, perhaps not even by Jesus Christ Himself.

It began to appear, for that matter, that perhaps Christianity had not been born in Bethlehem, but that it had been born much earlier, out there on the lonely, desolate, rugged shores of the Dead Sea.

TWO

On May 20, 1941, Edgar Cayce was "asleep" in his home at Virginia Beach, engaged in a reading that was being conducted by his son Hugh Lynn. This reading was uniquely different from others. Over the years, Edgar Cayce had, during Life Readings, made frequent references to the Essenes, a group about which, his son attests today, the man had no conscious knowledge. It was decided, therefore, that a series of readings should be done on the Essenes themselves in order to collect some information about them for students of history and religion.

Early in the reading, Hugh Lynn Cayce asked: "What is the correct meaning of the term 'Essene'?"

Edgar Cayce said: "Expectancy."

Exegetes generally agree that the earliest Biblical reference to a Messiah is in Genesis 3:15. In this passage, the Lord God is addressing the serpent which tempted Eve to eat the apple. The language differs in various Bibles but, in general, it is: "And I will establish a feud between you and the woman, between your seed and hers; (it or she) is to crush your head while you do lie in wait at (its or her) heel." Whether "it" or "she," the reference,

23

exegetes agree, is to the "seed" of Eve, the first woman, in the personage of Jesus Christ. The Edgar Cayce readings, as will be shown, present this idea in a different but not contradictory light.

The expectancy of a redeeming personage is mentioned frequently in the Bible, usually indirectly. For example, to Abraham the Lord God said: "In thee all the races of the world shall find a blessing." This is interpreted as meaning that the redeemer would be a descendant of Abraham. Abraham is considered to be the first Hebrew; to him it was revealed that there is one God. Abraham, his son Isaac, and Isaac's son Jacob all regarded Canaan as the land of the Hebrews, though they did not all live there themselves. While the Hebrews were in Goshen, in northeast Egypt, Jacob (who was also called Israel) divided the Hebrews into twelve tribes, naming his sons to head the tribes.

To his son Judah, Jacob said: "Judah, thou art he whom thy brethren shall praise; thy hand shall be at the neck of thine enemies; thy father's children shall bow down before thee . . . The sceptre shall not depart from Judah, nor a lawgiver from between his feet, until he comes who is to be sent."

Canaan was later partitioned by tribes by Joshua, successor to Moses after the Exodus, and to the Tribe of Judah went the area that now includes Jerusalem, Bethlehem and the Dead Sea. Solomon was of the Tribe of Judah. So was David. Speaking through the Prophet Nathan, the Lord God told David to build Him a house where His people could settle, and He said:

"And when thy days be fulfilled and thou shalt sleep with thy fathers, I will set up thy seed after thee, which shall proceed out of thy body, and I will establish his kingdom. He shall build a house for my name and I will establish the throne of his kingdom forever. I will be his father and he shall be my son."

Mary, the mother of Jesus, was of the House of David. So was Joseph, her husband. So important was this genealogy that it comprises the first passages of the Gospel, establishing the lineage from Abraham to Jesus and allowing the first Christians to claim that Jesus was the expected Messiah promised to Abraham.

24

Placing these events in time would be difficult—impossible, in fact. According to the Jewish calendar in use today, God created the world—and the Adam and Eve—about 5730 years ago. That would be about 3761 B. C. In terms of science, this is hardly acceptable. Archaeologists have determined that early Homo sapiens were living in the caves of Mount Carmel at least 35,000 years ago. In South Africa, scientists have found bones belonging to a species of Homo erectus that lived 3.5 *million* years ago. Factors like these contribute to the conflict between science and religion, with the weight of truth moving increasingly to the side of science. Clearly, some modifications in religion become necessary, and some have been made. For example, Pope Pius XII stated that it was up to the individual Roman Catholic to believe either in Evolution or in Divine Creation as depicted in Genesis; but, he said, Catholics were required to believe that at some point God gave Man his soul. The Edgar Cayce readings deal with this matter, but with a different resolution.

According to the readings, God did create the world in the evolutionary pattern suggested in Genesis. But the process did not take six days; it took, say, six eons. Man became a product of this evolution. But God did not give Man his soul. Souls took men unto themselves.

During the Exodus, God told Moses that His name was Yahweh, meaning "I am who am." Now that Yahweh was filling His promise to make Canaan the land of the Jews, only Yahweh was to be worshipped there. But things did not work out that way. Canaan, approximately the former Palestine, was already occupied by Semitic peoples of various backgrounds. There were kings and priests in their palaces and temples, with their own governments and gods. Thus the Jews had to fight their way into their homeland and they had to fight to keep it. And they fought amoung themselves. Soon after the twelve tribes were settled in Canaan, around 1035 B. C., they argued among themselves, with those in the north forming the Kingdom of Israel and those in the south forming the Kingdom of Judah. Neither kingdom could avoid being profoundly influenced by the cultures already existing all around them, any more than they could avoid wars with them. For that matter, there were times when each Jewish kingdom allied itself with pagans in wars against the other.

The influence became even more intimate when Ahab, prince of Israel, married Jezebel, princess of Phoenicia and worshiper of Baal, chief of the pagan gods. When Ahab became king, it was Jezebel, as queen, who really ruled the country. She imported hundreds of Baal priests and installed them on Mount Carmel, which overlooks the Mediterranean at what is now the city of Haifa. The mass invasion of idol worshipers into the land of Yahweh stirred the wrath of the Prophet Elijah. Since Elijah holds an important position in the philosophy which has evolved from the Edgar Cayce readings, this:

He was born around 876 B. C. at Tishbeh in Gilead. The town no longer exists, but the region was to the southeast of the Sea of Galilee. Early in life, he felt called to serve Yahweh. He spent his youth in the desert, fasting, wearing rough, shaggy clothes. He lived for a while in a cave on Mount Carmel, where there was a school of prophets. It was a house of study, actually. Besides their spiritual exercises, the prophets made copies of the sacred books for posterity. From time to time they traveled across the countryside, joyously acclaiming that Yahweh was God.

It was to displace these men and to dilute their religion that Queen Jezebel sent the Baal priests to Mount Carmel. The Yahwists either left to save their lives or they were killed. In time, only Elijah remained on the mountain. When Elijah left, he went in anger to Samarai, to the palace of Ahab, and he said to the king: "You are going to have to make up your mind which foot you're going to dance on. Either you are a Yahwist or a Baalist."

Strongly influenced by his wife, Ahab was unable to make up his mind, and so a contest was agreed upon. Two bullocks were taken to Mount Carmel and placed on altars. A great crowd watched as the priests gathered at one altar and called upon Baal repeatedly to prove his godship by setting the animal on fire with a flame from heaven. Nothing happened. Then Elijah stepped to his altar and put the same request to Yahweh. Immediately great flames appeared over the altar and the bullock was

26

quickly burned to ashes. The people cried out: "Yahweh is God! Yahweh is God!" And the Baal priests were killed. The Yahweh prophets returned to Mount Carmel.

Infuriated by the setback, Jezebel intensified her persecution of Yahwists. Elijah announced that Yahweh would punish her by bringing a three-year drought upon the land, and this happened. During the drought, Yahweh kept Elijah in food by having ravens bring him bread and meat every morning. In Zarophath, Elijah was fed by a widow whose food he miraculously multiplied and whose son he returned from the dead.

Throughout his life, Elijah fought the pagan invasion of Israel. Through his influence, new men rose to power in Jerusalem and Damascus, and they eventually overcame the threat by conquering the country.

Elijah chose as his disciple Elisha, a well-to-do farmer. Elisha also lived at Mount Carmel for a while, and it was he who accompanied Elijah to Jericho. The time had come for Elijah to complete his sojourn in this world, and they both knew it. At the Jordan, Elijah parted the waters with his mantle, which, it was said, was the source of his powers. And then he gave the mantle to Elisha. There appeared to them a chariot of flames, drawn by horses of flames. Elijah boarded the chariot and was borne away into the sky in a great wind.

The school of the prophets remained on Mount Carmel as the centuries unfolded toward Christ. Other things in the country changed a great deal. At times, even the attitude toward the expected Messiah changed. Yahweh's chosen people had their eras of glory, but again and again the country was conquered by its enemies, the cities were leveled, the people enslaved. Perhaps for this reason the attitude developed among many Jews that the expected Messiah would come as a great king who would unite the people and lead them to ultimate and lasting triumph. Even some of the prophets referred to him in this way. With time, the Messiah took on the role of an anticipated national hero in many minds.

With time, too, three "parties" or sects developed in the country, and they were all in existence when Jesus Christ was born. The most numerous group were the Pharisees. When, about two hundred years before Christ,

27

the spiritual leaders of Judea became lax, the pious Jews who continued to adhere strictly to the commandments became known as Assideans, which was derived from the Hebrew word Hasidim or Chassidim, meaning pious. When the Maccabees family organized a revolt against the leaders, the Assideans joined the fighting; but when the revolt became more political than religious, the Assideans withdrew. When the Maccabees devolved into the Hasmoneans, the Assideans became known as Pharisees— separatists—and they were persecuted. Though Queen Alexandra was Hasmonean, she favored the Pharisees. Under her reign, they were the real leaders of the country, a position they retained after the Roman occupation in 63 B. C.

Priests, laity and most of the scribes were Pharisees. In addition to believing in Mosaic Law, they believed that interpretations of the Law by the scribes were equally valid. They placed religion above politics, feeling they could live with any government which did not restrict religious freedom, and for this reason they not only got along well with the Romans, but had even asked the Romans to take over the country during the Hasmonean dynasty. Believing that Yahweh was their king as well as God, many Pharisees experienced conflict in paying tribute to their pagan conquerors, and it was Jesus who told them to render unto Caesar the things that were Caesar's and unto God the things that were God's. Pharisees believed in the immortality of the soul, retribution in the afterlife, the resurrection of the just, angels, spirits and Divine Providence. They accepted the doctrine of God's cooperation in human acts; they also believed in free will and moral responsibility. They believed that the Messiah would restore the Davidic dynasty and free Jews from foreign domination.

Another of the three parties at the time of Jesus were the Sadducees. Never numerous, they were nevertheless influential because tneir members included the nobility, the wealthy and the higher ranking priests. At the time of the Roman occupation, the high priest of the Sanhedrin was a Sadducee. Scholars regard the Sadducees as more Hellenistic than Hebrew. One reason may be that whenever life at home became too restrictive most Sadducees could afford to go to the countries to the north, where there was already a heavy Hellenistic influence. The Sadducees, for example, did not believe in retribution or resurrection. They held to the Sheol concept: there was a place in the earth where the dead went, without judgment. Sadducees did not believe in angels or spirits. They accepted the Mosaic Law but not the scribal interpretations. While the Sadducees rejected answered prayer, Divine guidance and Divine Providence, they did accept free will.

Some exegetes see the Sadducees as the spiritual heirs of the Priest King Melchizedek, who blessed Abraham and was paid tithes by him. That the father of all Israel should pay homage to Melchizedek suggests to some experts that the priest-king was the precursor of the personage mentioned in Psalms who would be a King of Israel and a priest after the order of Melchizedek, the same personage identified in the Epistle to the Hebrews as Jesus Christ. By tradition, Melchizedek did not die but was raised to heaven. At the time of Jesus, the Sadducees did not accept the idea of a Davidic Messiah because David was post-Mosaic and not mentioned in the Torah, the first five books of the Bible. Any belief they might have had in a priestly Messiah was probably diluted by their Hellenistic contacts for generations. To the Pharisees, Jesus of Nazareth could not have been the Messiah because He had come on to the public scene as a carpenter instead of a king; to the Sadducees, He was a political rabblerouser who had to be crushed in order to protect their own position.

It is puzzling to students of history and students of religion that the third party or sect in existence at the time of Jesus is not mentioned in the New Testament at all—the Essenes. Both the Pharisees and the Sadducees repeatedly come under criticism by the authors of the New Testament, but there is not a word about the Essenes, good or bad. The discovery of the Dead Sea Scrolls and the excavation of the house of studies at Qumran have stirred considerable conjecture about the Essene role in Judea at the time of Jesus but there has been little agreement. There has been, in fact, some disagreement as to the meaning of the word Essenes itself.

Some scholars feel that Essenes and Assideans have the same derivation—Hasidim: pious. Others associate the term with Hassaim—silent. Other suggestions: the bathers, the builders, the men of action, the chaste, the vision-seers. In any event, it can hardly be an accident, a coincidence or an oversight that the Essenes are absent from the pages of the Bible. Josephus Flavius (A. D. 37-100?), the Jewish historian, rated the Essene sect in the same category with the Pharisees and Sadducees. A Pharisee himself, he lived at an Essene house of studies for a year; and in his appraisal of the three sects, the Essenes clearly get the most sympathetic treatment.

What happened, then?

What was there about the Essenes that perhaps led the authors of the New Testament to ignore them?

On the other hand, what was there about the Essenes that perhaps led subsequent editors of the New Testament to edit them out?

The Metropolitan Samuel could not find a buyer for his scrolls. He had a contract with the American School of Oriental Research, in Jerusalem, to publish photographs of his scrolls, and he was to receive half the profits. After five years in the U. S., the contract had brought him less than five hundred dollars. Exhibits in museums had brought him a bit more. The main roadblock to the sale was the complaint by the Jordanian Department of Antiquities that the scrolls were stolen property. Though no legal action was instigated, the Jordan government warned the Metropolitan of such steps if he tried to return to his monastery, then in the Arab held section of Jerusalem. As things were, buyers evidently were not interested. Another roadblock was the fact that publication of the photographs decreased the value of the scrolls. Certainly, as antiquities, the scrolls were a treasure; but scholars who might otherwise have pressured universities or museums to buy the scrolls for them to study could now study the pictures, and thus this pressure did not develop. For five years, then, the scrolls spent most of the time in a safety deposit vault in a bank in Hackensack, New Jersey, where Metropolitan Samuel was living in an Assyrian neighborhood.

In the summer of 1954, General Yigael Yadin came to the United States to raise funds for Israel. He knew, of course, that the scrolls were here. For him they held great value not only in terms of science and scholarship but mainly in terms of history: they were documents written by his forefathers. Reportedly, Yadin wrote to Metropolitan Samuel and did not get an answer. This would be understandable. Yadin was a Zionist Jew; the Metropolitan was a Christian Arab. Then a strange thing happened. This ad appeared in the *Wall Street Journal:*

THE FOUR DEAD SEA SCROLLS
Biblical Manuscripts dating back to at least 2000 B. C. are for sale. This would be an ideal gift to an educational or religious institution by an individual or group.

Keeping himself in the background, General Yadin used intermediaries to negotiate the purchase at a price of $250,000. At first, the Israeli government provided $150,000, with the rest coming from the American Fund for Israeli Institutions; but then D. Samuel Gottesman, a New York businessman, repaid both sources and offered the scrolls as a personal gift to Israel. Sometime over the next several months, the scrolls were taken secretly to the Hebrew University in Jerusalem and into the care of Professor Sukenik. The Metropolitan Samuel, meanwhile, had placed the money into a trust which was to be administered by members of his church for religious and educational projects.

On February 13, 1955, the Israeli Premier Moshe Sharett announced that all the scrolls taken in 1947 by the Bedouins from what had become known as Cave One at Wadi Qumran were now reunited at Hebrew University and would be put into a special museum to be called the Shrine of the Book.

There were, in all, eleven scrolls; but they comprised seven manuscripts, and it is for this reason that they are called the Seven Dead Sea Scrolls. Actually, there were only six compositions, since two of the scrolls, one obtained by the Metropolitan and the other by Sukenik, are the same—the Book of Isaiah. But these scrolls, priceless though they are, are only a fraction of additional scrolls and fragments which were subsequently found in other caves at Qumran and elsewhere along the western shores of the Dead Sea.

After the news got out about the first findings in the caves, the Jordanian government closed off the entire area and turned it into a military zone. The only people allowed freedom of movement in and out of the zone were the Bedouins of the Ta'amire tribe. They were given, in a sense, a monopoly on cave-hunting into history, and they have flourished on it. Over the years, they have brought in all or parts of over four hundred manuscripts, from which scientists have pieced together the entire Old Testament except the Book of Esther. Many non-Bible documents have been found, and, in a way, they are of even greater value. By agreement with the government, the Bedouins continued taking their finds to the cobbler Kando in Bethlehem, who in turn sold them to the Jordanian-owned Palestine Archaeological Museum in Old Jerusalem. In twenty years, close to $500,000 was paid, though nobody knows how much of it reached the Bedouins. The money came in part from the Jordanian government and in part from museums and foundations interested in the research.

Oddly enough, there has never been enough money. Buying the fragments from the Bedouins obviously has been costly; but there have been other expenses that can run equally high, for services that are equally important. The experts who can piece the fragments together and translate them are a rare breed. Most of them have been university professors, usually with families to support, and in order to earn a living they must give the majority of their time to teaching and writing. The financial support that would enable these men to devote their talents wholly to the scrolls has not appeared. It has been pointed out by some experts that religious institutions, which, it would seem, should have a vital interest in the scrolls, have actually paid little attention to them and provided little, if any, support. Though some of the expert scientists who have worked on the scrolls have been clergymen, they have also been so few in number that they will never live to finish the vast amount of work that still remains to be done. What has been needed all along has been a bigger staff, which means bigger money.

One expert, Professor John Marco Allegro, of Manchester University, England, has intimated that perhaps the indifference is actually an apprehension of what the scrolls may reveal. In *Harper's Magazine*, August, 1966, he stated:

"The very scholars who should be most capable of working on the documents and interpreting them have displayed a not altogether surprising, but nonetheless curious, reluctance to go to the heart of their matter. The scholars appear to have held back from making discoveries which, there is evidence to believe, may upset a great many basic teachings of the Christian church. This in turn would greatly upset many Christian theologians and believers. The heart of the matter is, in fact, the source and originality of Christian doctrine."

Edgar Cayce would have gone along with that.

Edgar Cayce said: "I do not make any claims for myself. I do feel from experience that through the readings, as may be obtained through me from time to time while in an unconscious state, those lessons, those suggestions, are presented which, if applied in the inner life of the individual to whom they are directed, will give a clearer, a more perfect understanding of physical, mental and spiritual ills. But you must judge for yourself. Facts and results are the measuring rods."

Edgar Cayce was his own best measuring rod.

He was born on March 18, 1877, on a farm in Western Kentucky, and it was a Sunday. One day when he was still a small boy he went out to the nearby woods to watch a log-chopper at work. The man jokingly remarked that he had the strength of Samson. The boy did not know what that meant, so he asked. The man explained that he had attended a revival meeting the previous evening, at which the preacher spoke about the strengths God could give people, as He had given Samson the strength to destroy a building with his bare hands, thus beginning the liberation of Israel from the Philistines. Intrigued, young Edgar went home and asked his mother to read him the story from the Bible. Locating it in the

33

Book of Judges, she read it to him, and he thought it was the most exciting thing he ever heard. From then on, he often asked his mother to read the Bible to him. When he was old enough to be taken to church, it was the Bible stories the preachers told that held him in utter fascination. He started school when he was seven.

When he was ten and could read, he asked for and was given a Bible of his own. In the woods, at a bend of the stream, was a quiet, lonely place where he could spend all the free hours his life allowed him, and he would read the Bible. One evening that summer, a guest happened to disclose that he read the Bible through completely once a year. Edgar admired this. There and then he vowed that not only would he, too, read the Bible once a year for the rest of his life, but he would also begin that night reading it rapidly to make up for the years of his life he had already lived. It took him over two years to catch up with himself.

On a May afternoon of his thirteenth year, Edgar was again at his favorite place in the woods, now into the thirteenth reading of his favorite book. He had reached, perhaps by chance, the Book of Judges, and he was reading the story of Samson, the first Bible story he ever heard. Suddenly he became aware that he was not alone. He looked over his shoulder, into the sunlight, and he saw a woman. At first he thought that it was his mother, fetching him for his chores. Then he realized that it was someone else, and it seemed that she had wings on her back.

She said: "Your prayers have been heard. Tell me what you would like most of all, so that I may give it to you."

He stared at her in disbelief for what seemed a long time, and then he said: "Most of all I would like to be helpful to others, and especially to children when they are sick."

The woman vanished.

Edgar went home and told his mother what had happened, and he asked: "Do you think I've been reading the Bible too much? It makes some people go crazy, doesn't it?"

She took his Bible from him and read from the Gospel of John: " 'Verily, verily, I say unto you, Whatsoever

34

ye shall ask the Father in my name, He will give it to you. Hitherto have ye asked nothing in my name; ask, and ye shall receive, that your joy may be full.' " Then she looked at him. "You're a good boy; you want to help others. Why shouldn't your prayers be heard? You don't have to stop reading the Bible. I'll know if something goes wrong with you. But I think we'd better not tell anyone about this, for now."

He did not tell anyone for years. But a strange thing happened the next day.

Though young Edgar enjoyed reading the Bible, he did not enjoy reading his school books and so he was not a good student. His school was just a country school; his teachers were usually an uncle or an aunt; for a while, his own father taught there; many of his fellow students were relatives. Edgar seemed to be the dullard of the family. That day, he did not know a single word of his spelling assignment. The teacher, his Uncle Lucian, made him stay after school and write the words over and over. Edgar was late getting home to his chores; and when his father found out why, the man was furious. Cayce later recalled:

"In the evening, I had the same hard time in preparing my spelling lesson. I studied it and each time felt that I knew it; yet when I handed the book to my father and he gave me the words to spell, I couldn't spell them. After wrestling with it for two or three hours, receiving many rebuffs for my stupidity, something inside me seemed to say, 'Rely on the promise.' I asked my father to let me sleep on my lesson just five minutes. He finally consented. I closed the book and, leaning on the back of the chair, went to sleep. At the end of five minutes, I handed my father the book. I not only knew my lesson but I could then spell any word in the book— not only spell the words but could tell on what page and what line the word would be found. From that day on I had little trouble in school, for I would read my lesson, sleep on it a few minutes, and then be able to repeat every word of it.

"I could not explain this ability. It was a wonder to my parents, my associates and my teachers. I did not attempt to reason why this happened. Today, my life is a combination of literally thousands of such experiences. Although I understand many of the laws associated with these phenomena, my understanding is born of experience, and I leave the technical explanations to others."

Edgar Cayce quit school at fifteen, having completed six years of education. He worked on his father's farm for two years, then moved into town—Hopkinsville—to get a job and try to save some money for whatever his future held for him. At the time, he was thinking of becoming a missionary. In town, he worked in a stationery-bookshop for over four years. By then he had met the girl he wanted to marry, and he realized he would have to have a far better income in order to do so. He applied for a job with the Louisville wholesaler who was supplying the Hopkinsville store, and he was hired. Louisville put Cayce on an economic treadmill for two years: the more he earned, the more life cost him. At Christmas, 1899, he quit the job and went home. His father was then selling insurance on the road for a fraternal organization and suggested that Cayce join him. Cayce also agreed to work as a traveling salesman for the Louisville wholesaler.

In March, 1900, Edgar Cayce was working in Elkton, a town about forty miles from home. Lately he had been suffering headaches, some of them severe, and one day while working his head began to pain so badly he thought it would split. He called on a doctor and received a sedative, which he took on returning to his hotel. Next thing he knew, he was at home in his own bed. He learned that a Hopkinsville friend had come upon him in the Elkton railroad station, wandering about in a daze, and had brought him home. Two doctors were in the room; and when Cayce tried to answer their questions, he found that he could not speak. Examining him, the doctors concluded that he had caught a bad cold from walking around Elkton without a hat or coat on a wintry day, and they said that with rest and liquids he should soon be all right.

He was all right the next day, but he still could not speak above a whisper, and the effort was painful. A week later, he was up and about and restless to get to work, but still he could not speak in his normal voice.

Another week passed. Another. Cayce was examined by Dr. Manning Brown, the county throat specialist; and when the doctor could not detect any reason for the loss of voice, he asked if other specialists might try to diagnose the condition. The specialists came, one after another, weeks passing, and Edgar Cayce remained unchanged.

He came to the conclusion that his condition was incurable. As long as he did not try too often to speak in his whisper the pain was less when he did whisper. He felt he could live with that. Unable to talk, however, he would be unable to do any selling. Of necessity, he had to look for another job. He found one as assistant to a photographer in Hopkinsville, and he learned the trade. The circumstances which led to Cayce's cure were either a stroke of luck or an act of God.

A year passed. Dr. Brown would not give up. From time to time he sent other specialists to the Cayce home, but they could find nothing organically wrong with Edgar. Then a vaudeville hypnotist came to town. There had already been newspaper articles out of New York, from a Dr. John F. Quackenboss, to the effect that hypnotism would one day be used to cure illnesses. Thus when the vaudevillian came to Hopkinsville, some of Cayce's friends went to him to ask what he could do. The man was willing to try. The experiment was conducted in Dr. Brown's office. To everyone's amazement, Cayce, while hypnotized, spoke in his normal voice, but upon being awakened he could speak only in the whisper. The experiment was repeated several times, always with the same result.

Present at one of the tests was William Girao, professor of psychology at South Kentucky College. Local papers had carried items about the experiments; Girao sent the clippings to Quackenboss in New York and suggested that he examine Cayce himself. When Quackenboss arrived in Hopkinsville, he put Edgar Cayce into a deep trance and then gave him the post-hypnotic instruction that upon awaking he would speak in his normal voice. But Cayce did not react to the order to wake up. He slept for twenty-four hours. When he finally awoke, he still spoke in a whisper. And then for a week he could hardly sleep at all.

From New York a bewildered Quackenboss sent Girao the only explanation he could imagine for the unusual development. He said that, looking back on the experiment, he had the feeling that there was a point when he no longer had control over the hypnotized Cayce. It was as though Cayce himself had taken over. Quackenboss suggested that Cayce be hypnotized again and then be informed that he, Cayce, was in control. This way, he might remember what had happened to him to bring on his condition, and then maybe doctors would find out what therapy to apply.

The only available person in Hopkinsville with the ability to hypnotize was a bookkeeper by the name of Al Layne, and he had taught himself the feat from a correspondence course. Because of this, Cayce's parents were reluctant to let him experiment with their son. But Edgar wanted to try.

"You know," he said in his whisper, "I don't think anybody has really hypnotized me at all. I put myself to sleep, the way I do on books. Let's do it that way. Then we can give Dr. Quackenboss's idea a chance—have somebody talk to me. Al Layne can do it."

On the afternoon of Sunday, March 31, 1901, Al Layne arrived at the Cayce home. Waiting for him in the living room were Edgar Cayce and his parents. They told Layne how they wanted to conduct the experiment and, though disappointed that he would not be able to display his talent, Layne agreed to the plan. Cayce lay down on the sofa and put himself to sleep. When his breathing became slow, deep and steady, Layne leaned toward him.

"Edgar," he said, "this is Al Layne. I want you to do what I tell you. I want you to envision your body. Take a look at it. You know you have something wrong with your throat. Tell us what it is. And speak in your regular voice."

Cayce mumbled in his sleep, then said, clearly and in his own voice: "Yes, we can see the body." There was a movement of his closed eyes. Then: "In the normal state, this body is unable to speak, due to a partial paralysis of the inferior muscles of the vocal cords, produced by nerve strain. This is a psychological condition producing a physical effect. This may be removed by increasing the

38

circulation of the affected parts by suggestion while in this unconscious condition."

Taking the cue, Layne said: "The circulation to the affected parts will now increase and the condition will be removed."

Almost immediately, a blush came upon Cayce's face, gradually deepened, then gradually spread to his neck and chest. His father opened his shirt to make him comfortable. For twenty minutes, the three others sat there, watching him. Except for the fierce redness of his skin, he seemed all right, deep in a peaceful sleep. Then he cleared his throat and said: "It is all right now. The condition is removed. Make the suggestion that the circulation return to normal and that after that the body will awaken."

Layne said: "The circulation will return to normal. The body will then awaken."

Gradually Cayce's skin took on its normal color. He awoke, sat up, coughed, and then he grinned. He said: "It is all right now."

It was his first reading.

Next day, he did his second reading—on Layne. Not a well man, Layne looked older than his thirty-five years. Curious about the body that had caused him so much discomfort, he had studied osteopathy by mail and later obtained a license to practice. During the reading, Layne was amazed by Edgar Cayce's knowledge of anatomy. Cayce not only told Layne about ailments he knew he had but also described others that came as a surprise to him. And the therapy recommended during the reading worked.

Layne brought others to Cayce. In the small town which Hopkinsville was at the time, it was impossible to keep secret this incredible new faculty Edgar Cayce had acquired. Articles appeared in the town paper, then the county paper, then the state and national. Letters appealing for help began to arrive from all over the country. Looking back, Cayce once said:

"I was still ashamed to talk about these readings. People thought me odd and I resented for a time the little slights and slurs of my associates who took pleasure in laughing at me. It is hard to be 'different.' I finally selected photography as a life work and gave only my spare time and evenings to the increasing number of requests for readings. It was only when I began to come in contact with those who received help from following the suggestions given in readings that I began to realize the true nature of the work which lay before me. Indeed, I did not even decide to give my whole time to this work until results in my own family brought me face to face with facts.

"One day a man phoned me at my studio: 'I have heard of what you, with the assistance of a certain man, have been able to do for those who are very sick. I have a little girl whose condition is said to be hopeless. Won't you come and see what you will say about her condition?'

"I will never forget my feelings on that occasion. I journeyed to the little city where this professor lived. He met me at the train with his carriage, drove me to his home, introduced me to his wife, then asked me if I would like to see the little girl and examine her. How foolish I felt! I didn't know whether I wanted to or not. I knew that of myself I could tell nothing. I knew I had never studied anything of the kind and didn't know what it was all about. I told him: 'Yes, but I do not suppose it makes any difference.' They led me into a room where the little girl was sitting on the floor rolling blocks. A nurse was attending her. She looked as well as any child I had ever seen, and I couldn't imagine what in the world would be said regarding such a perfect looking little girl."

As it turned out, the eight-year-old had been suffering numerous convulsions daily since the age of two, and a series of doctors had been unable to do anything for her. During the reading, Cayce reported that congestion had formed at the base of the girl's brain following an attack of influenza at the age of two and had worsened with each convulsion. Osteopathic treatment cleared the condition and the girl began a normal life.

As gratifying as such experiences must have been for Edgar Cayce, he remained puzzled and disturbed, and on a number of occasions he wanted to stop the readings. But the appeals kept coming in. At first, Al Layne served as conductor, putting the questions to Cayce. When Layne left for formal osteopathy studies, Cayce's father took over. In 1903, Edgar Cayce married Gertrude Evans, to whom he had been engaged for six years, and eventually she became the principal conductor for the rest of his life. In those first years, the readings dealt almost entirely with the diagnosis of disease and recommendation of therapy, but occasionally a reading took an unusual turn. For example, a New Yorker who had received a copy of his reading notified Cayce that he could not locate a supply of the medicine Cayce had recommended. Cayce did another reading and was able to inform the man which drugstore in New York had the medicine. When the man replied that the store didn't have it, Cayce did another reading and was able to describe exactly where in the shop the bottle was located. It was there; it had been there so long that the druggist had forgotten about it.

Over these first years, a pattern in Cayce's therapeutic recommendations developed, the significance of which remained elusive. Often, as with the New Yorker, Cayce would recommend a medicine which hadn't been produced commercially for so long that pharmacists either forgot about it or never heard of it. Other times, he would recommend the use of herbs or roots which, if their medicinal value had ever been acknowledged, had long since been abandoned as witch-doctors' brews. Also, this period was decades before the popularity of "natural" or "health" foods, but Cayce recommended them. It would seem, then, that available to Edgar Cayce during readings was a vast knowledge of medicinal chemistry by which people cured themselves long before pharmacology became a science. Thus the possibility that other areas of knowledge might also be available to Cayce somehow eluded everybody. Cayce himself did not think of it until he was almost fifty years old, and the idea was not his own.

In 1915, Edgar Cayce went to Lexington to do a follow-up reading on a woman whose severe arthritis had diminished by therapy elicited at earlier sessions, and he was introduced to a neighboring family, the Kahns. The Kahns had a son, Leon, who was not well. Cayce did a reading on the boy. The results were so effective that, in gratitude, the Kahns decided that as a family they would give Edgar Cayce all the support they could.

41

The eldest son, David, then fifteen, was made responsible for the project. At the time, the Kahns were in the grocery business; there wasn't much they could do for Cayce. But then, Cayce himself wasn't sure what ought to be done. Next time they talked about it, Edgar Cayce knew.

David Kahn served in World War I, returning to Lexington in 1919, a captain. He also returned a zealous Edgar Cayce missionary. While he had been away, doctors refused to continue the therapy which Cayce's reading had recommended for Leon Kahn, and the boy had died. David Kahn did not want that to happen again to anybody else. During the war, he had talked to many friends about Edgar Cayce. Intrigued, they now all wanted to help. He told Cayce this at their reunion meeting.

"I'm sure I can raise the money for you," Kahn said. "What do you need?"

"A hospital," Cayce said.

It was the first time he had thought of it, but instantly he knew perfectly well that a hospital was what he needed. Leon Kahn had not been the only person to die because doctors scoffed at the readings' recommendations. And in many instances when the readings were carried out successfully, doctors scoffed because no scientific records had been kept of the case and so nothing could be proved. Edgar Cayce did not want to prove anything. All he wanted was a place where the readings could be executed in the most sanitary conditions, with the most modern equipment, and by qualified doctors. Scientific records would be kept, of course, and they could speak for themselves. For Cayce, the only value in such records was to put trust into the validity of the readings, not in him as a man. For himself, he wanted nothing.

David Kahn couldn't wait to get started. He suggested that he and Cayce make a tour of the country, using the friends he had met in the war to help arrange public demonstrations of Cayce's faculties to raise money for the hospital. By this time, Edgar Cayce was operating his photographic studio in Selma, Alabama, and his second son, Edgar Evans Cayce, had been born. The tour, then, meant both a financial and personal loss for Cayce, taking him away from his business and, from time to time, his family. The tour took him westward across the South, then north into the Wheat Belt, then east. Though a success for Cayce himself, the trip was not sufficiently remunerative, and it became clear that another way to raise funds for the hospital would have to be found.

The way that was suggested left Edgar Cayce considerably uneasy. It was suggested that, since Edgar Cayce had located in a New York drugstore a bottle of medicine nobody knew was there, he should be able to locate in Texas oil deposits which nobody as yet knew were there. At first, Cayce balked at this. He had always refused to engage in experiments which involved profits for anyone, including himself. But when he was assured that profits from the oil venture would go to his hospital, he felt it was admissible to make an exception in this case. With Kahn and others involved, he headed for Texas. Oil was indeed located, but something always went wrong in the process of bringing it up—machinery would break, a fire would occur, a storm would wreck equipment.

Hugh Lynn Cayce, then a teen-ager, spent a summer with his father in Texas, conducting the readings, and he wrote his mother that he was puzzled by the frequency with which his father said during readings that the oil venture was doomed to failure unless everyone involved was "in accord" with the purpose of the project: the profits were for the hospital. Hugh Lynn knew that a profit was what was left over after all expenses were paid, and he wondered if anyone involved in the project might be planning on such huge expenses that there would be little left over for the hospital. The project never got that far; funds ran out and the effort was abandoned. Between the tour and the oil project, it was four years before Edgar Cayce and his family were again settled in Selma.

It had so happened that on the tour Cayce had given a demonstration of readings in Dayton, Ohio, and present at some of them had been a businessman by the name of Arthur Lammers, a man with a long, profound and active interest in things philosophical, metaphysical and occult. Impressed by the Dayton readings, Lammers had an idea he wanted to put to Cayce. Because of Cayce's immediate travels on the tour and his subsequent travels in Texas, over two years passed before Lammers was able to locate him in Selma and go to him there. Lammers's idea was intriguing.

Lammers had observed that some of the medical recommendations during health readings turned out to be accepted medical practice in centuries long past, and now Lammers wondered if perhaps information on other areas of past centuries might also be available to Edgar Cayce during readings. For example, what about the origin of the planet? What about the evolution of man? What about the nature of souls? What about the divinity of Jesus Christ? What about life after death?

Cayce was disturbed by these questions. A Christian, he accepted the Bible's answers for these unanswerable questions. He felt it would be unwise—even dangerous —to delve into such spiritual areas. He was confident that his psychic faculties were God-given, but who could tell whether they might become Satan-used. Anyway, Cayce doubted that his faculties were meant for such purposes. Conceding that such ideas had never occurred to him before, he was sure that the effort would not work.

Lammers pressed him to try. There was so much to be learned; and because the readings might take time, Lammers invited Cayce to do them in Dayton with all expenses paid plus an attractive per diem. Cayce didn't care about the money. Whatever the true reason behind the Texas fiasco, Cayce concluded from it that diagnosis of illness was the limit of his powers. As for money, people for whom Cayce was doing readings by mail had developed the habit of sending him donations out of gratitude, and some of the doctors who consulted him would send him checks for professional services. Cayce's current plans, then, were to phase himself out of photography so that he could devote himself fulltime to what he now called the "work." Toward that end he had hired a secretary, Gladys Davis, who was to work with him for the rest of his life. And the ultimate end remained, of course, the hospital.

And yet Cayce could not dismiss a nagging uncertainty about Lammers's idea. If there were some past truths— some eternal truths—which through the readings could be made known and serve for the betterment of people, where would he stand in the eyes of God if he refused to let himself be used for this purpose? He put the question to Gertrude, but she was as uncertain as he was. They finally agreed however, that he should at least give it a try, depending on God to let him know through the readings whether he was doing the right thing.

One morning in 1923, Edgar Cayce opened the door of his room in a Dayton hotel to Lammers, Lammers's male secretary Linden Shroyer, and a public stenographer. Because Lammers had witnessed readings, he knew how to conduct one. They did not know where to begin, so Lammers suggested that Cayce give him a horoscope reading. Cayce laughed; he did not believe in astrology. But he said: "I'm ready. Ask me anything you want." And he went to sleep.

When he awoke an hour later, he found himself looking into the astonished faces of three staggered people. After they told him what he had said, he, too, was staggered. This was Edgar Cayce's first Life Reading. Over the next twenty years, he was to do thousands more. Out of them came a pattern of life that made Life far different for thousands of people, for they learned that this life was not the only life they ever had or ever will.

THREE

In weaving the tapestry which relates Edgar Cayce to the Dead Sea Scrolls and their time, it becomes pertinent now to look to a man of his own time: Pierre Teilhard de Chardin, Frenchman, Jesuit, paleontologist. *The Texas Catholic Herald,* February 21, 1969, contains an article by Father William D. Steele, with this headline: "Edgar Cayce; did he contact de Chardin's 'universal mind'?" This:

45

"Cayce was not an educated man in the ordinary sense of the word. He was a sixth-grade dropout. He claimed that while asleep he was in contact with the Universal Mind or Universal Consciousness of mankind. The contact was made through his own subconscious mind and revealed during the many 'readings' Cayce gave while asleep. . . .

"Quite apart from the authenticity of Edgar Cayce's alleged communication with a universal mind, it is interesting to compare his thought with that of Father Teilhard de Chardin. Teilhard believed that the 'without' of reality, the external organization of reality, was directed by a 'within' which he describes as 'consciousness.' It is this 'within' of things that directs the course of evolution as manifested in the 'without' of things. Moreover, Chardin wrote that this 'consciousness' within all creation is steadily mounting in intensity.

"Teilhard believed that consciousness was intensifying not only in the individual man but in mankind itself collectively. He frequently writes of the 'collective consciousness' of the human race or the 'noosphere,' as he calls it. It is this 'collective mind of mankind' that bears an uncanny resemblance to the 'universal mind' with which Edgar Cayce was supposedly in contact."

Teilhard de Chardin was born about four years after Edgar Cayce was born and died about ten years after Cayce did. There is no evidence that the two men ever heard of each other. Hugh Lynn Cayce, who was undoubtedly closer to his father than any other man, did not himself come to know about Teilhard's work until the Frenchman's books started to become popular in the 1960s. Cayce died two years before the Dead Sea Scrolls were found. Teilhard died a few months before the first in-depth study of them was published for the general public—the long article in *The New Yorker* by Edmund Wilson in 1955. There had already been, however, several articles on the scrolls in the technical journals. Also, during 1949 and 1950 *The New York Times* published numerous articles on the debate among scholars on the age and authenticity of the scrolls, a debate which was dissipated when the techniques of modern science definitely placed the scrolls in the First Christian Century and before, and the excavation of the Qumran community definitely linked them to the Essenes. Quite likely, then, Teilhard, as a scientist specializing in things past, knew about the scrolls and was presumably interested in them, but whether he ever evaluated them in terms of his own thoughts about the nature of the past and the future is not known.

Both Cayce and Teilhard presented information—thoughts, perhaps—that could not have been made available to them through means available to everybody else. Cayce's means were, of course, the readings, always with witnesses present. Some of Teilhard's biographers refer to his having had "psychological experience," but the nature of it isn't clarified. The fact remains that these two men, whose lives were so different and whose concepts of Life differed, nevertheless came close to being of one conviction in so many ways.

Teilhard was born to a wealthy family near Clermont in South-Central France. To the age of eleven, he was educated at home by his parents and tutors. His father had made a hobby of the natural sciences; often the man and boy would stroll the family estate, the man teaching the boy the scientific names of trees and birds, rocks and stars. The boy acquired a lifelong interest in rocks. At twelve, he entered a Jesuit secondary school, a high school, where for the next five years he excelled in all his subjects except religion. He explained to his family that he found his other subjects interesting because they made him think, whereas religion bored him because he only had to memorize. And yet he was a religious youngster. At home, he attended daily Mass with his mother; at school, he attended daily Mass with the student body; the student clubs he joined were of a religious nature, with daily devotions. His parents expected him to go into the sciences; they were not surprised when he announced at seventeen that he wanted to become a priest-scientist. The surprise was his reason for putting the priesthood first: a desire for spiritual perfection. To Catholics, this is an attribute of mature sainthood one does not expect to hear from a boy.

He joined the Jesuits. In 1901, at twenty, he finished his novitiate and began his junioriate studies at Laval.

47

The following year, another State-Church crisis developed in France, and religious institutions were closed. Teilhard and his classmates moved to the Channel Island of Jersey. This delighted him: a new place meant new rocks to study. He was still a student when, in collaboration with a professor, he published his first scientific paper, on the rock formations of Jersey. Jesuit rules require an aspirant to teach for two or three years before the final studies which lead to ordination. Teilhard was assigned to teach sciences in a high school in Cairo, and he was also appointed custodian of the school's museum. The museum was a veritable scrapheap of antiquities, dumped there by previous priest-archaeologists who had made finds in the desert and then left them unidentified in the museum when they rushed off on new assignments. Sorting them, Teilhard displayed a natural genius for being able to pinpoint the age of any object made from rocks, this long before the development of modern techniques. It was in this way that several real treasures were identified that otherwise would have remained on a shelf gathering dust.

France still being closed, Teilhard went to England for his final studies for the priesthood, and he was ordained there on August 24, 1911, at the age of thirty. He expected to be sent on for further studies in science, but the political atmosphere changed in France and he was needed there for parish work. A year passed before his superiors broached the subject of further studies to him, and they left the choice of a speciality up to him. There was so much to learn that he could not decide, so he consulted a friend, who told him: "Prehistory and its allied sciences." It was a choice that would one day send shudders through the intellectual circles of the Catholic Church.

During World War I, Teilhard took time out from his studies to volunteer as a litter bearer in the French army. He saw action at Champagne, Verdun and Marne, and he was cited for bravery under fire. A friend chided him for the risks he was taking, warning that one of them might cost him his life, and Teilhard said: "Then I will merely change my state."

This was the first evidence that he had already been thinking of the concept of Life which has become known as Teilhardism, a concept which was to bring such personal anguish into his own life that years later he wrote to a friend: "Pray that I do not become bitter."

Edgar Cayce had more than one occasion to ask friends for the same prayer.

At some point never specified, Father Teilhard came to the conclusion that it was intellectually obligatory for him to put aside, at least in terms of time and circumstances, the Genesis delineation for the creation of the world. This must have been a painful experience for him as a devout Christian, and yet it was a necessity for him as a dedicated scientist. And yet he felt that these two sides of himself—and of life—were reconcilable. Science and religion would remain enemies as long as they remained strangers. Actually they could supplement each other, even complement each other, as the specifics of science clarified the speculations of religion.

Teilhard the Christian could not believe that it would take the Almighty God six days to do anything, including create the world and everything in it. God could have willed the world to be as a finished product by the mere thought of it in His mind. Teilhard the scientist knew that this was not the way it happened, nor was Genesis. From his higher studies of archaeology, geology, anthropology and paleontology, and perhaps through his psychological experiences, he reached the conviction that Man, even Pre-man, did not come into being on a single occasion in one place. Scientists were digging up too many fossils of Man and Pre-man in too many different places too far apart and of too many archaeological ages. Either Man—or Pre-man—was a terrific traveler or he came into being more than once and in many places and at different times and in various circumstances.

Then where did everybody go? Some lines of Man or Pre-man extinguished the species by continuing to mate with other animals whose morphogenetic bent was in some other direction. Other lines were wiped out by every imaginable natural catastrophe. Some withered away because of a lack of progeny, especially of the same type but of different sexes. Still others were victims of the same diseases and ailments and conditions and

49

accidents that are still killing people today. How then to explain the fact that today's Man is, despite certain superficial differences, anatomically and physiologically just about the same wherever you found him? Through the natural selection implicit in evolution, this evidently was the form and function which survived against the challenges of change of the millenia. How then to explain the different races? Early breeding habits, prolonged in-breeding, environment, the immobility of the masses. Arrange a massive transmigration and encourage interracial breeding and the present racial structure would become dissolved and disappear.

Father Teilhard came to believe that God did not *make* the world—He started it off, for reasons of His own and with evolution as His intention and perfection as His goal. Each level of evolution constituted a state, each state higher than the one before. Teilhard often said: "Man did not descend from apes. He ascended." Integral to each ascent to the higher state was a force of convergence, just as, in the formation of the planet, elements converged into gases, gases into metal and rock. Inanimate things and animals were acted upon by the force. Man alone could act upon the force itself because Man alone had free will. When did he get it? Teilhard could not name the date but he could name the moment. It was the moment when Pre-man looked around at his world and experienced awareness for the first time. At that moment, the consciousness of self came into being, and animal became Man. He could observe, he could appraise, he could decide. He could think. As a being, he was the ultimate in evolution. But he was not the end of the line.

Among the things Edgar Cayce and Pierre Teilhard de Chardin had in common was the treatment they received from people who either did not understand them or made no effort to understand them. Cayce was repeatedly called a crackpot and a charlatan by the press. He was arrested twice—once in New York and once in Detroit —on charges of fraud, but both times the charges were dropped because they could not be proved. There was nothing Edgar Cayce could do but proceed in privacy, dignity, humility and honesty. Teilhard had a rougher time. As a Jesuit, he had a vow of obedience to his superiors, who were numerous. As a Jesuit, he also had a vow of obedience to the Pope, which could mean anybody who had influence on the Pope. Whether Teilhard could proceed was, therefore, not up to him. And he was stopped.

When, after World War I, Teilhard began teaching in Paris, he would occasionally introduce into his lectures some of his thoughts which encompassed both science and religion. His students were fascinated, but his confreres were appalled. By dismissing Genesis, he was, they accused, ineluctably dismissing Adam and Eve as the first humans created by God, and by this he was also dismissing Original Sin. Students of Teilhardism are divided on this point. Some suggest that he intimated that Original Sin was some early theologian's explanation for the existence of evil in the world. Others say he conceded to Original Sin as some sort of disobedience in the past but that he could never come up with an explanation for it that satisfied him.

Another complaint against Teilhard were certain attributes he ascribed to Jesus Christ. He accepted Christ as consubstantial of the Godhead, but his convictions about the origin of Man and his doubts about Original Sin kept him from accepting the Redemption as the purpose for the Incarnation. Teilhard held, in effect, that Christ took on the experience of being man so that men could proceed to the experience of becoming Christ and that this, too, had always been implicit in evolution.

The way this would come about was another complaint against Teilhard. Father Teilhard believed that consciousness—thought—was, in a sense, a dimension: a state, and, as such, subject to convergence. Man, confronted by a decision, thought and then acted. When the thought was influenced by love and the decision resulted in action which contributed to the common good, then evolution took another step forward toward its goal: perfection. But when man decided against love and acted in selfish interest, then the convergence toward goodness was interrupted and all men suffered for it.

In Revelations is this: " 'I am the Alpha and Omega, the beginning and the ending,' saith the Lord, 'which is

51

and which was and which is to cóme, the Almighty.'" Teilhard took this to mean that just as all things emanate through Christ so do they proceed to Him as the ultimate. The Incarnation, then, was the factor which spirited Man on the right course for the perfection—the Christification—of the world by his thoughts, words and deeds.

Father Teilhard realistically acknowledged the existence of pain and wrong in the world, but he rarely referred to them in his writings. He considered them the negative side of the positive picture of progress implicit in evolution. As he put it, one talks about the height of the mountain, not the depth of the valley. Pain and wrong, he believed, were part of the evolutionary process, necessary to it, and as, through thought and love, man overcomes the remaining imperfections of the world, they will disappear. He also believed that when men acted against thought and against love—when they sinned—they were delaying the disappearance of pain and wrong from the world because they were acting against each other. Evil, he said, is the refusal of unity, integration, and the love of God.

In Teilhardian terms, thought encompassed research —the pursuit and organization of knowledge for the good of mankind and the unification of the world. Out of this came one of the most difficult Teilhardian ideas to grasp. He believed that the process of accumulating knowledge was intrinsic to evolution, that just as, during evolution, the planet acquired a layer of metal, a layer of rock, a layer of water, so it was acquiring a layer of knowledge resulting from the creative thinking of man. Teilhard called the layer the noosphere, *noos* being the Greek word for mind. Thus each discovery or invention or decision or compromise that contributed to the betterment of life and the improvement of human relations added to the noosphere, a slowly expanding envelope around the planet that will one day embrace it, bringing man to the threshold of the Omega.

In Teilhardian terms, the second factor involved in man's persistent advance on perfection was love: Christian love: Christianity. When both thought and love covered the world in the noosphere, evolution would be complete;

it could then be said that God's world had been created, and it would be His.

The Edgar Cayce readings produced a similar theory of evolution, but with intriguing variations. Just as Cayce had never studied medicine, he had never studied the natural sciences or comparative religion. His "information," as he called it, came during Life Readings, and it abounded with scientific and religious details which should ordinarily have required a lifetime of study. To follow through on Father Steele's observation in the *Texas Catholic Herald*, regarding the "uncanny resemblance" between Cayce's Universal Consciousness and Teilhard's noosphere, if there is any association between the two at all it could be conjectured that Cayce while asleep had contact with the growing envelope of knowledge resulting from the thought and love of everyone who had ever contributed to it since the consciousness of self turned animal into Man.

All things, according to the readings, are expressions—extensions—of God. All things are, in a sense, of the same wavelengths, and it is because of the limitless variety of combinations of wavelengths that one thing differs from another. Souls are extensions of God, and the wavelength combination which makes souls unique is free will, which no other expression of God has. God made souls for companionship, and He made all souls at one time. A soul knows it is of God, but also of itself and also of every other soul. This condition of unity with God and yet separateness from Him gives the soul its consciousness and allows for the companionship. A soul is both masculine and feminine, both positive and negative, both aggressive and responsive.

As long as souls remained obedient to God, they shared in His knowledge and wisdom. As such, they participated with Him in Creation, which came about in the way that is now acknowledged to be evolution. Some souls enjoyed this experience so much that, while it was going on, they tried to influence it with their own wills. They tried to be God. This was the Great Disobedience. This was the Fall of the Angels. This was the birth of ego. This was the birth of guilt. It also caused these souls to be separated from God, to go out into the evolving world and become part of it.

Until then, these souls had been of the spirit and of the mind—the subconscious mind. Now part of the physical world, they acquired a conscious mind in order to participate in the consciousness of things. One way souls participated was to enter a thing and take on its essence. What these things were depended on where in the solar system the souls chanced to be, evolution proceeding differently on each planet. During each occupation, the soul's conscious mind suppressed its subconscious mind, separating the soul more and more from the Eternal Consciousness. Souls, as such, being hermaphroditic and eternal, do not procreate; but if the thing being occupied was a living creature which did procreate, the soul participated in the act, taking either the male or female role, depending on the gender of the creature, and, if female, reproducing the creature. When the creature died, the soul was liberated, in a sense, its subconscious resumed supremacy; and the soul could then proceed to its next occupation. What these souls were actually seeking was a way back to God.

God knew this. Because He had known certain souls would disobey and would then search for a return, He had included the means for the return in His Divine Plan. But He left it to souls to find it. Their longing search took them through all the solar systems and their dimensions. Our solar system has eight dimensions, of which Earth is the third. It was here that some of the souls came upon the creatures which seemed best suited for them—the early anthropoids. The souls, using their subconscious faculties, influenced the apes physiologically in a way that changed their animal behavior and sent them off on a different evolutionary projection. As their behavior changed, so did their appearance. The moment came when they were no longer animals but Pre-man. Then the souls entered them and occupied them. This could have been the Teilhardan moment of awareness, the moment of consciousness of self that made animal Man.

As a soul entered the human it had chosen it knew what was expected of it by God. It was to lead a human life in the way God expected an obedient soul to live. The soul's subconscious desired this; but, upon inhabiting the human, the subconscious was repressed, as with any other animal, and the soul functioned with its conscious mind. The subconscious made its presence known, sometimes in terms of conscience, sometimes in terms of inspiration, sometimes in dreams. But the conscious mind reigned, and this mind was constantly tempted by the animal instincts and urgings of the body. For a soul, exercising its free will, to resist every temptation was extremely difficult, as every human being has learned. The soul which succeeded could move on to the next dimension en route to God. The soul which failed would, upon death of the body, have to try again in another body. However, certain credits, as it were, could be accumulated in each incarnation and eventually result in success; and these credits could be any thought, word or deed which God could accept as good, in terms of morality, justice or the betterment of mankind, for as such they were free-will extensions of the goodness of Himself.

The first generations of humans were keenly aware of what was happening. Being able to procreate, they did so in order to provide more bodies for souls waiting to inhabit them. The waiting soul chose which body to enter. The soul's subconscious, learning from mistakes of the past sojurn, would seek a new life in circumstances which offered a better chance for progress toward spiritual perfection. Once born, however, the same conflict began, and the outcome could be decided by the sensitivity of the conscious to the subconscious. Sometimes, because there had been progress, a soul chose to return to the same family, the same walk of life, the same way of life. Other times, the soul would go into some other dimension for a period of time before returning to Earth. The Edgar Cayce Readings suggest that only one soul succeeded in each dimension on the first try, and that soul was the entity now called the Christ. Concerned about other souls, all part of His, He took human form again and again to give spiritual assistance and spiritual guidance to those still on the voyage.

As generation followed generation, there were periods when the true nature of what was going on became so dimmed to the conscious that people wondered where they had come from, why they were here, where they were going. It was from the lonely subconscious that ideas of the truth seemed to seep through, and people began to organize religions. Actually, it is only over the past five or six hundred years that Man has become rather well acquainted with his planet, and wherever explorers or scientists or missionaries have gone they have found some semblance of a religion. In each religion, there was something of the others. This led to the probability that isolated peoples once had contact with others, which was true in many cases. But the common factor was not actual contact. It was the subconscious in each soul, pressing through upon the conscious whenever possible, reminding. Another thing that happened was that, from time to time, a great soul, again at the threshold of God, would have in its consciousness much, even all, of the knowledge and wisdom of the subconsciousness, and the human being inhabited by the soul could do marvelous things—heal, raise the dead, read minds, reveal the past, disclose the future. This was not always a welcomed wonder. Such souls could cause panic among people. They could disrupt the established order, threaten existing religions. It was not uncommon for these men to be killed, for their followers to be exiled, for any writings about them to be destroyed or be put in a secret place where they could be read only by men of "maturity," say, who would not be swayed by them. The terrible result of this was that the Divine Plan of God would be thwarted by a few at great cost to many.

According to the Cayce readings, the five races appeared simultaneously but in different places at the moment souls entered bodies. The white race began in the Carpathians. The black race appeared in East Africa. The yellow race began in the Gobi Desert. The red race began in Atlantis. The browns appeared in the Andes. According to the readings, the surface of the planet was different then. The east coast of the U. S. was the lowlands of Atlantis. The west coast of South America was the west coast of Lemuria. The Mississippi delta was ocean. The Sahara was fertile. So were Persia and the Caucasus, where the Garden of Eden was. The Nile emptied into the Atlantic. The North and South Poles were tropical. Pertinently, around the turn of the century, a German scientist by the name of Alfred Wegener came up with the idea that the world's land was once one vast continent which had broken up and drifted apart into the present continental structure, and for this he was widely ridiculed. As scientific technology improved, however, scientists began to believe that originally there had been two continents—Gondwanaland (comprised of South America, Africa, India, Australia and Antarctica) and Laurasia (North America, Greenland and Eurasia). More recently, scientists found themselves looking with favor on Wegener's theory, that there was one land mass, which he called Pangea, and that it began breaking up some 200,000,000 years ago. Supporting evidence appeared early in 1970 when the fossil remains of an animal once common in Africa were found in Antarctica. Because the animal, the hippopotamus-like reptile called Lystrosaurus, couldn't possibly have swum between the two continents, scientists concluded that the two land masses had been connected long ago. Then, in March, 1970, other pertinent evidence was discovered. Two Harvard scientists, studying marine life off the coast of Cuba, found at a depth of twenty thousand feet a growth of a type of coral which had never before been found lower than five hundred feet. They concluded that the coral had been connected to a land mass which, for unknown reasons, had sunk four miles to the bottom of the sea. In light of the Cayce readings, this would be Atlantis, which would one day rise again, causing much of the U. S. east coast to sink into the sea.

According to the readings, the Christ soul took human form six times in order to show the consciousness of souls the life that must be led as humans for them to complete their sojourn in this dimension. He came as Enoch and as Melchizedek, neither of whom was born or died. Then He decided that a personal example would be more effective and thereafter He was born of woman. He was Joseph, He was Joshua, He was Jeshua, He was Jesus.

The life that the Christ soul wanted humans to lead was a life of simplicity and service, which was probably why it was so difficult. Ego expects this conduct of others but is reluctant to give it. The Cayce readings expressed the pattern this way:

"Know that thyself, in its physical state, is a part of the plan of salvation, of righteousness, of truth, of the Creative Forces, or God, in the earth.

"Each person is a corpuscle in the body of that force called God. Each person is a manifestation of the Creative Force in action in the earth. Each person finds himself with a body that seeks expression of itself and a mind capable of becoming aware of what the body presents, what other men present, and what influences are acting upon the body and upon the mind itself. Each soul enters the material plane not by chance but through the grace, the mercy, of a loving Father, that the soul may, through its own choice, work out those faults, those fancies, which prevents its communion and at-one-ness with the Creative Forces. As to whether a soul is developed or retarded during a particular life depends on what the person holds as its ideal and what it does in its mental and material relationships about that ideal.

"Life is a purposeful experience, and the place in which a person finds himself is one in which he may use his present abilities, faults, failures, virtues in fulfilling the purpose for which the soul decided to manifest in the three-dimensional plane. Know in thyself that there are immutable laws and the universe about thyself is directed by laws set in motion from the beginning.

"So, as ye condemn so are ye condemned. As ye forgive, so may ye be forgiven. As ye do unto the least of thy brethren, so ye do it unto thy Maker. These are laws; these are truths; they are unfailing. And because He may often appear slow in meting out results does not alter or change the law. An error, a fault, a failure must be met. Though the heavens, the earth, may pass away, His word will not pass away. His word is the way, the truth, the light. Each soul must pay to the last jot or tittle.

"How can-ye do His bidding? Not in mighty deeds of valor, not in exaltation of thy knowledge or power, but in the gentleness of the things of the spirit: love, kindness, longsuffering, patience. These thy Elder Brother, the Christ, has shown thee, that thou, applying them in

58

thy associations with thy fellow man day by day, here a little, there a little, may become one with Him as He has destined that thou shouldst be. Wilt thou separate thyself? For there is nothing in earth, in heaven, in hell, that may separate thee from the love of thy God, of thy brother, save thyself.

"Then be up and doing, knowing that as thou hast met in life those things that would exalt thy personal self these ye must lose in gentleness, in patience. For in patience ye become aware of your soul, your individuality lost in Him, your personality shining as that which is motivated by the individuality of the Lord and Master. Thus does your destiny lie within yourself, and the destiny of the world.

"Hold fast to that faith exemplified in thy meditation, in thy counsels, in thy giving out to thy fellow man. For he that hides himself in the service of his fellow man through the gifts, through the promises as are in Him, hides many of the faults that have made him afraid through his experience in the earth. For it is not what one counts as knowledge that is important, nor what one would attain in material realms, but what one does about that which is known as constructive forces and influences in the experience of thyself and thy fellow man. For, as He has given, 'As ye do it unto others, ye do it unto Me.' He is the way, the life, the light. He is the Creator; He is the giver of all good and perfect gifts. Man may sow, man may act in material manifestations, in matter, of spiritual forces, yet the returns, the increase, must come from and through Him who is the gift of life. It is not a consideration of where or even how the seed of truth in Him is sown; for He gives the increase if it is sown in humbleness of spirit, in sincerity of purpose, with an eye-single that He may be glorified in and among thy fellow man. This is the way, this is the manner, that He would have thee follow.

"Let thyself, then, become more and more a channel through which His manifestations in the earth may arise, through thy efforts, in the hearts, the minds, of thy fellow man. For mind—in man, to man—is the builder, ever. That, then, must be directed, given, lost in the singleness of purpose, that there may come the greater awaken-

59

ing within the consciousness of thy fellow man that HE is in the earth, that His words are as lights to men in dark places, to those that are weak, to those who stumble. For He will give thy efforts that necessary force, that necessary power, to quicken even those that are asleep in their own selfishness, in their own self-indulgences, and bring to their awakening that which will make for glorious activities in the earth.

"Keep, then, the faith thou hast had in Him; for He is thy strength, He is thy bulwark, He is thy Elder Brother. In Him, ye may find that which will bring to thee, and others, joy, peace, happiness, and that which makes men not afraid. For He is peace, not as men count peace, not as men count happiness, but in that harmonious manner in which life, the expression of the Father in the earth, is one, even as He is one.

"Keep the faith."

Certainly it must have been faith which helped both Edgar Cayce and Father Teilhard to survive the long sufferings that plagued their lives. Both were men of simplicity and service, never seeking anything for themselves. Cayce was once offered a thousand dollars a day if he would don a turban and a robe and do his readings behind a curtain, traveling about with bodyguards and in expensive cars, all to give him a flair of mystery. He refused. Cayce never earned more than a hundred dollars a week in his life, and there were many weeks when he didn't earn anywhere near that. Teilhard, as a Jesuit, had a vow of poverty. He had no income at all and could not even claim that he owned anything in his own name. Neither man argued with his critics. Cayce wouldn't; Teilhard couldn't. Neither man defended the thoughts that emanated from their minds. Cayce couldn't; Teilhard wasn't allowed to. Neither man sought to establish a cult, and yet cults grew around them both, growing larger and more vocal after their deaths. In human terms, Cayce was probably the luckier man. In the darker moments, Cayce had his family. Teilhard had only his work. But both men had God, so both men went on.

Edgar Cayce's friendship with David Kahn had survived the Texas misadventure. Readings indicated that Kahn should go to New York and enter the furniture business; he did, and he was successful. It was through Kahn that Cayce came to know Morton Harry Blumenthal, a New York stockbroker, whose ear ailment was improved after a physical reading. He had a Life Reading done and was soon wrapped up in the Cayce work. Learning of Cayce's wish for a hospital where therapy suggested during readings could be carried out, Blumenthal offered to back it. Readings had repeatedly indicated that the hospital should be built at Virginia Beach. But it was to be more than a hospital. The Life Readings were, of course, of value to the individuals for whom they were done, but they were also producing views into history which time had clouded over and, perhaps, men had tried to shut out. The readings became of value, as well, to people interested in all spheres of history. Because of their nature, they were also of interest to students of psychic events. The establishment at Virginia Beach would, therefore, also be a study center. It became a university.

On May 6, 1927, a charter of incorporation was granted by the state of Virginia to The Association of National Investigators, the purpose of which was to engage in general psychic research and to provide for the practical application of any knowledge obtainable through the medium of psychic phenomena. A year later, the thirty-bed Edgar Cayce Hospital stood on a hilltop at the north end of Virginia Beach and was receiving patients. A few months after that, the Atlantic University was nearby, ready for students. And a year after that, the stock market crashed. Blumenthal could no longer afford to underwrite the Association until it became self-supporting, and thus the entire organization had to be discontinued. In June, 1931, at the request of a number of his friends, Edgar Cayce organized The Association for Research and Enlightenment, and it was to proceed with the same work but on a more modest scale. The Cayce home was the headquarters and Hugh Lynn Cayce became the administrator. With the exception of occasional blasts in the press, it was by word of mouth that the Association grew slowly but steadily, occupying Edgar Cayce fulltime for the rest of his life. After his death in 1945, people thought that the Association would be dissolved. Instead, interest in the readings continued a steady growth, not only because of their intrinsic value but also because of a growing need in many people for answers that seemed available only in the realm of the psychic and occult. In 1955 it became necessary for the Association to seek larger headquarters, and the building that was acquired was the one on the hilltop that had been the Edgar Cayce Hospital.

Interest in Teilhardism surged after his death because it was not until his death that his books could be published. When, after World War I, Teilhard began teaching prehistory sciences in Paris, he would from time to time inject some of his own explanation of evolution into his lectures. His students were fascinated, but his confreres were appalled. He was, they said, teaching heresy. At first, Teilhard tried to answer the complaints with further discussion, but he got nowhere. Then he allowed his lectures to be mimeographed so that the objectors would have something specific to debate instead of generalities. Copies of the lectures began popping up all over Paris, usually in student groups, and soon it was impossible to get another person into the crowded classroom whenever Teilhard spoke. Students began to quote him in their classes on religion. Before long, the faculty was in an uproar. Teilhard insisted that in his effort to reconcile religion and science he was not dealing in theology, but his superiors did not interpret his writings that way. Under ordinary circumstances, it would have been a simple matter for a religious superior to silence a troublemaker by reminding him that he had a vow of obedience and must do what he was told. But this could not be done easily with Teilhard. He was already a giant in science. He was popular at the university, where his views were well known. His family had national stature. To dispose of him discreetly, his superiors decided he could do with some field work in his special field. They sent him to China.

For the rest of his life, Teilhard was never in Paris for more than a few months at a time. Every time he returned, his cult would revive, there would be controversy again, and he would be sent away. Between 1923 and 1946, he was mostly in China. At the beginning,

China was just opening its doors to the scientists of the world, and they were rushing in from every major country. Like many of them, Teilhard believed at the time that Man may first have appeared in Asia, and so, though he knew he was in exile, he was happy to be among the pioneers. He made many valuable finds while in China, the most important of which was the skull of a prehuman who had lived 360,000 years ago. This was the Peking Man, and it was, for a time, the oldest fossil known; much older fossils were later found in Africa.

Teilhard achieved something else in China that was equally important, and, in a way, equally important scientifically. From the start, there had been fierce nationalistic competition among the groups of scientists, each nation trying to surpass others. In Teilhardan terms, research, the pursuit of knowledge and thus thought, was supposed to be unifying and convergent, in fact as well as in essence. Without knowing it, then, the scientists were defeating their whole purpose. Teilhard often said of himself: "I am not a Frenchman, I am not a Chinaman, I am not an American. I am an Earthan." Surrounded by a competitive and, in this case, disunifying atmosphere, Teilhard pointedly called on the various groups regularly, impressing them with the scope of his scientific knowledge, charming them with his modesty and gentle wit, openly telling them how his work was going, and, with seeming naivete, asking them about theirs. Disarmed, they told him. He gave dinner parties regularly, inviting men from the various groups, knowing that out of professional courtesy each would have to reciprocate in kind. Gradually he broke down the nationalistic disunity. The excavation which produced the Peking Man was an international effort, headed by Teilhard. It can be said that the international cooperation in scientific research today, particularly in the field of geophysics, is the outgrowth of Teilhard's efforts to get scientists to contribute to the noosphere, the Omega, whether they believed in that ultimate or not.

Teilhard wrote. As a Jesuit, his writings had to be submitted to his superiors for approval before publication. His strictly scientific works were approved; anything bordering on his theory of evolution was not. Teilhard spent the war years in China. Unable to do field work, he spent his time writing. When, in 1946, he was able to leave, his departure was so sudden and travel space so restricted that he had to leave most of his writings behind. With the country in a civil war which ended in a Communist mainland, his papers disappeared and were never found again. Another great loss was the skull of the Peking Man. During the war, the Japanese put the skull, plus other fossils, on a ship bound for Tokyo, but the ship was sunk at sea by American bombers. Centuries from now, some scientist will find that ship and he will examine the bones of the men who went down with it, and he will forever wonder how in the world it happened that one member of the crew appears to be 360,000 years older than the others.

In Paris, Teilhard gave his surviving writings for typing to Jeanne Mortier, a friend who voluntarily served as his secretary for many years. As his superiors were considering the work, copies began to appear throughout Paris and the cult arose again. The result was that in 1947 Teilhard was notified by his superiors in Rome that none of his theoretical writing could be published in his lifetime. He was thus silenced. Furthermore, to get him out of Paris, he was summoned to Rome and put to work in the Jesuit archives writing the history of the Order. This was a great waste that fortunately was shortlived. French scientific organizations, both government and professional, asked that he be returned to Paris so that they could honor him for his work in China. The request could not be refused, and Teilhard received just about every French honor there was. After this, he clearly could not be sent back into hibernation in the library. He found himself making trips to Africa, visiting anthropological sites, and he came to the conclusion that Man had actually originated there. He also visited South America, and he became a consultant to a New York foundation which sponsored anthropological expeditions. Though he could not publish on his theory, he hadn't been told that he could not write about it, and he continued to do so. In view of the treatment he was getting, it would not have been surprising if he had left the Jesuits, even left the Catholic Church, but this was unthinkable for him. In the first place, he had joined the Jesuits not for science but for spiritual perfection. Also, breaking his vows would have been, for him, a negative act, an act of disunification, and this would have been against everything he believed about the forward-moving, converging world.

One day a Jesuit friend told him: "If I were you, I'd see that somebody else had copies of all these scripts you're writing. If the Order gets hold of them after your death, that'll be the end of them." Teilhard sent copies to Jeanne Mortier, as he sent copies of everything he wrote for the rest of his life. In Paris, Jeanne Mortier had quietly organized a foundation in Teilhard's name so that others could take care of the writings in case she died first. Teilhard died of a heart attack in New York on Easter Sunday, 1955. A few months later, Jeanne Mortier gave the manuscript of *The Phenomenon of Man* to a French publisher. Great pressure came from Church circles to prohibit the publication of the book, including the threat of putting it on the Index, but the book came out and created a storm. Two years later, *The Divine Milieu* was published, and there was another storm. That year—1957—the Vatican banned Teilhard's books from the libraries of Catholic institutions around the world. In 1962, the Vatican issued a *monitum*—a formal warning—against "ambiguities and even grave errors" in his writings, which was one step short of putting him on the Index.

Today, the storms which developed over Edgar Cayce and Father Teilhard have subsided.

Today, in the parking lot of The Association for Research and Enlightenment at Virginia Beach are "MD" license plates from all over the country, as physicians are in the library studying the Cayce physical readings. Also in the library are clergymen of all faiths and professors of all subjects, all of them seeking information on the things Edgar Cayce believed.

Today, Teilhard's books are in Catholic institutions. Seminars on Teilhardism are held in Catholic universities, attended by clergymen of all faiths and professors of all

subjects, all of them seeking information on the things
Pierre Teilhard de Chardin believed.

It is significant that prominent Catholics are members of The Association for Research and Enlightenment.
It is significant that the best-attended lecture one year
at Union Theological Seminary, New York, was on Teilhardism, given by a former president of the seminary who
had known Teilhard personally.

Each year, October through May, week-long seminars
are held at Virginia Beach, attended by people of all
faiths. Repeated surveys consistently show that their two
main areas of interest are:

How to pray.

And how to meditate.

Edgar Cayce and Father Teilhard were ecumenists long
before most people heard of the word.

And the Essenes were ecumenists long before them.

FOUR

There are now variances in what is known about the
Essenes, variances brought about by differences in the
writings about them in their own time, by what has been
learned from the Dead Sea Scrolls, and by what was disclosed during Edgar Cayce readings. The contemporary
writings provide a good foundation for an understanding
of all that has happened since. Writing around A. D. 20,
Philo of Alexandria, the Jewish philosopher, said this:

"They were a sect of Jews, and lived in Syria Palestine,
over 4000 in number, and called Essaie, because of their
saintliness; for *hosio*—saintly, is the same word as
Essaeus. Worshipers of God, they yet did not sacrifice
animals, regarding a reverent mind as the only true
sacrifice. At first they lived in villages and avoided
cities, in order to escape the contagion of evils rife therein.

They pursued agriculture and other peaceful arts; but accumulated not gold or silver, nor owned mines. No maker of warlike weapons, no huckster or trader by land or sea was to be found among them. Least of all were any slaves found among them; for they saw in slavery a violation of the law of nature, which made all men free brethren, one of the other.

"Abstract philosophy and logic they eschewed, except so far as it could subserve ethical truth and practice. Natural philosophy they only studied so far as it teaches that there is a God who made and watches all things. Moral philosophy or ethic was their chief preoccupation, and their conduct was regulated by their national (Jewish) laws. These laws they especially studied on the seventh day, which they held holy, leaving off all work upon it and meeting in their synagogues, as these places of resort were called. In them they sat down in ranks, the older ones above the younger. Then one took and read the Bible, while the rest listened attentively; and another, who was very learned in the Bible, would expound whatever was obscure in the lesson read, explaining most things in their time-honored fashion by means of symbols. They were taught piety, holiness, justice, the art of regulating home and city, knowledge of what is really good and bad and of what is indifferent, what ends to avoid, what to pursue—in short, love of God, of virtue, and of man.

"And such teaching bore fruit. Their lifelong purity, their avoiding of oaths or falsehood, their recognition of a good providence alone showed their love of God. Their love of virtue revealed itself in their indifference to money, worldly position and pleasure. Their love of man in their kindliness, their equality, their fellowship, passing all words. For no one had his private house, but shared his dwelling with all; and, living as they did in colonies (the tasous), they threw open their doors to any of their sect who came their way. They had a storehouse, common expenditure, common raiments, common food eaten in Syssitia or common meals. This was made possible by their practice of putting whatever they each earned day by day into a common fund, out of which also the sick were supported when they could not work. The aged

67

among them were objects of reverence and honor, and treated by the rest as parents by real children."

Writing around A. D. 300, Eusebius, Bishop of Caesarea, and called one of the Fathers of the Church, said this:

"Even in our own day, there are still men whose only guide is God; men who live by the true reason of nature, not only themselves free but filling their neighbors with a spirit of freedom. They are not very numerous indeed. But that is not strange. For the highest nobility is ever rare; and then these men have turned aside from the vulgar herd to devote themselves to a contemplation of nature's verities. They pray, if it were possible, that they may reform our fallen lives; but, if they cannot, owing to the tide of evils and wrongs which surges up in cities, they flee away, lest they too be swept off their feet by the force of its current. And we, if we had a true zeal for self-improvement, would have to track them to their places of retreat, and, halting as suppliants before them, would beseech them to come to us and tame our life, grown too fierce and wild; preaching, instead of war and slavery and untold ills, their gospel of peace and freedom, and all the fullness of other blessings."

Around A. D. 70, Pliny the Elder, the naturalist, wrote:

"The Hessenes live on the W. side away from the shores (of the Dead Sea), out of reach of their baneful influences, a solitary race, and strange above all others in the entire world. They live without women, renouncing all sexual love. They eschew money, and live among the palm trees. Yet the number of their fellows (convenarum) is kept up and day by day renewed; for there flock to them from afar many who, wearied of battling with the rough sea of life, drift into their system. Thus for thousands of ages (strange to tell) the race is perpetuated, and yet no one is born in it. So does the contrition felt by others for their past life enrich this set of men. Below them lay Engadi, a town once second only to Jerusalem in its fertility and groves of palms. Now 'tis but one more tomb.. Next comes Masada, a fort on a rock, and, like the former, not far from the Dead Sea."

Josephus, who wrote between A. D. 75 and A. D. 85, went into greater depth about the Essenes, but he claimed to have lived among the Essenes for a while and was thus better acquainted with their life. Some of his account conflicts with those of his contemporaries, even somewhat with himself, but not with Cayce. In *The Wars of the Jews,* Josephus reported:

"For there are three philosophical sects among the Jews. The followers of the first of whom are the Pharisees; of the second the Sadducees; and the third sect, who pretends to a severer discipline, are called Essens. These last are Jews by birth, and seem to have a greater affection for one another than the other sects have. These Essens reject pleasures as an evil, but esteem continence, and the conquest over our passions, to be virtue. They neglect wedlock, but choose out other persons' children, while they are pliable, and fit for learning; and esteem them to be of their kindred, and form them according to their own manners. They do not absolutely deny the fitness of marriage, and the succession of mankind thereby continued; but they guard against the lascivious behavior of women, and are persuaded that none of them preserve their fidelity to one man.

"These men are despisers of riches, and so very communicative as raises our admiration. Nor is there any one to be found among them who hath more than another; for it is a law among them, that those who come to them must let what they have be common to the whole order, —insomuch that among them all there is no appearance of poverty or excess of riches, but every one's possessions are intermingled with every other's possessions and so there is, as it were, one patrimony among all the brethren. They think that oil is a defilement; and if any one of them be anointed without his own approbation, it is wiped off his body; for they think to be sweaty is a good thing, as they do also to be clothed in white garments. They also have stewards appointed to take care of their common affairs, who every one of them have no separate business for any, but what is for the use of them all.

"They have no certain city, but many of them dwell in every city; and if any of their sect comes from other places, what they have lies open for them, just as if it were their own; and they go into such as they never knew before as if they had been ever so long acquainted with

69

them. For which reason they carry nothing with them when they travel into remote parts, though still they take their weapons with them, for fear of thieves. Accordingly there is, in every city where they live, one appointed particularly to take care of strangers and to provide garments and other necessaries for them. But the habit and management of their bodies is such as children use who are in fear of their masters. Nor do they allow of the change of garments or of shoes till they be first entirely torn to pieces or worn out by time. Nor do they either buy or sell anything to one another; but every one of them gives what he hath to him that wanteth it and receives from him again in lieu of it what may be convenient for himself; and although there be no requital made, they are fully allowed to take what they want of whomsoever they please.

"And as for their piety toward God, it is very extra-ordinary; for before sun-rising they speak not a word about profane matters, but put up certain prayers which they have received from their forefathers, as if they made a supplication for its rising. After this, every one of them are sent away by their curators to exercise some of those arts wherein they are skilled, in which they labor with great diligence till the fifth hour. After which they assemble themselves together again into one place; and when they have clothed themselves in white veils, they then bathe their bodies in cold water. And after this purification is over, they every one meet together in an apartment of their own, into which it is not permitted to any of another sect to enter; while they go, after a pure manner, into the dining room, as into a certain holy temple, and quietly set themselves down; upon which the baker lays them loaves in order; the cook also brings a single plate of one sort of food and sets it before every one of them; but a priest says grace before meat; and it is unlawful for any one to taste of the food before grace be said. The same priest, when he hath dined, says grace again after meat; and when they begin and when they end they praise God, as He that bestows their food upon them; after which they lay aside their white garments and betake themselves to their labors again till evening; then they return home to supper, after the same manner; and if there be any strangers there, they sit down with them. Nor is there ever any clamor or disturbance to pollute their house, but they give every one leave to speak in his turn, which silence thus kept in their house appears to foreigners like some tremendous mystery, the cause of which is that perpetual sobriety they exercise and the same settled measure of meat and drink that is allotted to them, and that such as is abundantly sufficient for them.

"And truly, as for other things, they do nothing but according to the injections of their curators; only these two things are done among them at every one's own free will, which are to assist those that want it and to show mercy; for they are permitted of their own accord to afford succor to such as deserve it, when they stand in need of it, and to bestow food on those that are in distress, but they cannot give any thing to their kindred without the curators. They dispense their anger after a just manner and restrain their passion. They are eminent for fidelity and are the ministers of peace; whatsoever they say also is firmer than an oath; but swearing is avoided by them and they esteem it worse than perjury; for they say that he who cannot be believed without swearing by God is already condemned. They also take great pains in studying the writings of the ancients and choose out of them what is most for the advantage of their soul and body; and they inquire after such roots and medicinal stones as may cure their distempers.

"But now, if any one hath in mind to come over to their sect, he is not immediately admitted but he is prescribed the same method of living which they use, for a year, while he continues excluded; and they give him a small hatchet and the forementioned girdle and the white garment. And when he hath given evidence, during that time, that he can observe their continence, he approaches nearer to their way of living and is made a partaker of the waters of purification; yet is he not even now admitted to live with them; for after this demonstration of his fortitude, his temper is tried two more years, and if he appear worthy they then admit him into their society. And before he is allowed to touch their common food, he is obliged to take tremendous oaths; that, in the

71

first place, he will exercise piety toward God; and then that he will observe justice toward men; and that he will do no harm to any one, either of his own accord or by the command of others; that he will always hate the wicked and be assistant to the righteous; that he will ever show fidelity to all men and especially to those in authority, because no one obtains the government without God's assistance; and that if he be in authority, he will at no time whatever abuse his authority, nor endeavor to outshine his subjects either in his garments or any other finery; that he will be perpetually a lover of truth and propose to himself to reprove those that tell lies; that he will keep his hands clear from theft and his soul from unlawful gain; and that he will neither conceal any thing from those of his own sect nor discover any of their doctrines to others, no, not though any one should compel him so to do at the hazard of his life. Moreover, he swears to communicate their doctrines to no one any otherwise than as he received them himself; that he will abstain from robbery and will equally preserve the books belonging to their sect, and the names of the angels (or messengers). These are the oaths by which they secure their proselytes to themselves.

"But for those that are caught in any heinous sins, they cast them out of their society; and he who is thus separated from them does often die after a miserable manner; for as he is bound by the oath he hath taken and by the customs he has been engaged in, he is not at liberty to partake of that food that he meets with elsewhere but is forced to eat grass and to famish his body with hunger till he perish; for which reason they receive many of them again when they are at their last gasp, out of compassion to them, as thinking the miseries they have endured till they came to the very brink of death to be a sufficient punishment for the sins they had been guilty of.

"But in the judgments they exercise they are most accurate and just; nor do they pass sentence by the votes of a court that is fewer than a hundred. And as to what is once determined by that number, it is unalterable. What they most of all honor, after God Himself, is the name of their legislator (Moses); whom, if any one blaspheme, he is punished capitally. They also think it a good thing to obey their elders, and the major part. Accordingly, if ten of them be sitting together, no one of them will speak while the other nine are against it. They also avoid spitting in the midst of them or on the right side. Moreover, they are stricter than any other of the Jews in resting from their labors on the seventh day; for they not only get their food ready the day before, that they may not be obliged to kindle a fire on that day, but they will not remove any vessel out of its place, nor go to stool thereon. Nay, on the other days, they dig a small pit, a foot deep, with a paddle (which kind of hatchet is given them when they are first admitted among them); and covering themselves round with their garment, that they may not affront the divine rays of light, they ease themselves into that pit, after which they put the earth that was dug out again into the pit; and even this they do only in the more lonely places, which they choose out for this purpose; and although the easement of the body be natural, yet it is a rule with them to wash themselves after it, as if it were a defilement to them.

"Now after the time of their preparatory trial is over, they are parted into four classes; and so far are the juniors inferior to the seniors that if the seniors should be touched by the juniors they must wash themselves, as if they had intermixed themselves with the company of a foreigner. They are longlived also; insomuch that many of them live above a hundred years, by means of the simplicity of their diet; nay, as I think, by means of the regular course of life they observe also. They contemn the miseries of life and are above pain, by the generosity of their mind. And as for death, if it will be for their glory, they esteem it better than living always; and indeed our war with the Romans gave abundant evidence what great souls they had in their trials, wherein, although they were tortured and distorted, burnt and torn to pieces, and went through all kinds of instruments of torment, that they might be forced either to blaspheme their legislator or to eat what was forbidden them, yet could they not be made to do either of them, no, nor once to flatter their tormentors or to shed a tear; but they smiled in their very pains and laughed those to scorn who inflicted the torments upon them and resigned up their souls with great alacrity, as expecting to receive them again.

"For their doctrine is this:—That bodies are corruptible and that the matter they are made of is not permanent; but that the souls are immortal and continue for ever; and that they come out of the most subtile air and are united to their bodies as in prisons, into which they are drawn by a certain natural enticement; but that when they are set free from the bonds of the flesh, they then, as released from a long bondage, rejoice and mount upward. And this is like the opinion of the Greeks, that good souls have their habitations beyond the ocean, in a region that is neither oppressed with storms of rain or snow or with intense heat, but that this place is such as is refreshed by the gentle breathing of a west wind that is perpetually blowing from the ocean; while they allot to bad souls a dark and tempestuous den, full of never-ceasing punishments. And indeed the Greeks seem to me to have followed the same notion, when they allot the islands of the blessed to their brave men, whom they call heroes and demi-gods; and to the souls of the wicked the region of the ungodly in Hades, where their fables relate that certain persons, such as Sisyphus and Tantalus and Ixion and Tityus, are punished; which is built on this first supposition, that souls are immortal; and thence are those exhortations to virtue and dehortations from wickedness collected; whereby good men are bettered in the conduct of their life, by the hope they have of reward after their death and whereby the vehement inclinations of bad men to vice are restrained by the fear and expectation they are in, that although they should lie concealed in this life, they should suffer immortal punishment after their death. These are the divine doctrines of the Essens about the soul, which lay an unavoidable bait for such as have once had a taste of their philosophy.

"There are also those among them who undertake to foretell things to come, by reading the holy books and using several sorts of purifications and being perpetually conversant in the discourses of the prophets, and it is but seldom that they miss in their predictions.

"Moreover, there is another order of Essens who agree

with the rest as to their way of living and customs and laws but differ from them in the point of marriage, as thinking that by not marrying they cut off the principal part of human life, which is the prospect of succession; nay, rather, that if all men should be of the same opinion the whole race of mankind would fail. However, they try their spouses for three years; and if they find that they have their natural purgations thrice, as trials that they are likely to be fruitful, they then actually marry them. But they do not use to accompany with their wives when they are with child, as a demonstration that they do not marry out of regard to pleasure but for the sake of posterity. Now the women go into the baths with some of their garments on, as the men do with somewhat girded about them. And these are the customs of this order of Essens."

In his *Antiquities of the Jews,* Josephus reports this:

"Now there was one of these Essens, whose name was Manahem, who had this testimony: that he not only conducted his life after an excellent manner but had the foreknowledge of future events given him by God also. This man once saw Herod when he was a child and going to school, and saluted him as king of the Jews. Now at that time Herod did not at all attend to what Manahem said, as having no hopes of such advancement; but a little afterward, when he was so fortunate as to be advanced to the dignity of king and was in the height of his dominion, he sent for Manahem and asked him how long he should reign. Manahem did not tell him the full length of his reign; wherefore, upon that silence of his, he asked him farther, whether he should reign ten years or not. He replied: 'Yes, twenty; nay thirty years'; but did not assign the just determinate limit of his reign. Herod was satisfied with these replies, and gave Manahem his hand and dismissed him; and from that time he continued to honor all of the Essens. We have thought it proper to relate these facts to our readers, how strange soever they be, and to declare what hath happened among us, because many of these Essens have, by their excellent virtue, been thought worthy of this knowledge of divine revelations."

A matter of interest in these excerpts is the time factor.

By the present calendar, Philo wrote about the Essenes at the time that Jesus was about twenty years old, and yet he wrote about them in the past tense. Pliny and Josephus, who wrote between fifteen and twenty years of each other, both used the present tense. Eusebius, who wrote over two hundred years later, first quoted Philo in the past tense and then commented on men of his own time who led Essenic lives. And Pliny observed that the Essenes had perpetuated themselves without marriage for "thousands of ages." Regardless of other variances in the accounts, it would appear that the Essene sect had been around for a long time, was influential at the time of Jesus, and remained so for a long time after. Philo's estimate of their number—four thousand—may seem small, but it is known that the Pharisees, the strongest sect or party in Jesus's time, numbered only seven thousand. The puzzling questions linger: Why are the Essenes not mentioned in the Bible? Why are they not, as a sect, mentioned in the Seven Dead Sea Scrolls or on any of the thousands of fragments? Where did they come from? How could they have remained so uninvolved in the life of Jesus? Where did they go?

The Scrolls provide answers to some of the questions to a degree. So do the Edgar Cayce Life Readings. First, the Scrolls.

1. The St. Mark's Isaiah Scroll is the oldest of the seven, dated at approximately 250 B. C. Made of strips of leather stitched together, it is about twenty-five feet long and a foot wide. The text, which is complete, is in fifty-four columns of Hebrew. In content, it differs only slightly from the Masoretic text. The Hebrew word "masora" means "tradition" and, in this case, it applies to the scholars charged with the responsibility of determining that recopied versions of the Old Testament were accurate. The task was difficult. Written Hebrew was, at first, comprised only of consonants, and, unless the reader was already familiar with the text, there was always the risk of misinterpretation. To overcome this, scholars introduced grammatical markings into the word forms, indicating the missing vowels. Even this was not a complete safeguard. It has been established that some of the people who recopied sacred texts were not beyond in-

jecting their own interpretations, thus changing thought context and even actual circumstances. When, during the third and fourth centuries A. D., the Fathers of the Church put together the Bible as we know it today, they had available to them earlier Hebrew and Aramaic texts of the same event but which differed from each other, and so they had to depend on Divine Guidance in deciding which account was accurate. The Masoretic text considered accurate was compiled in the tenth century. The similarity between its Book of Isaiah and the St. Mark's Isaiah Scroll shows what tremendous detective work these scholars must have done to determine accuracy in this particular passage of the Old Testament.

2. The Hebrew University Isaiah Scroll, acquired by Sukenik, was probably written in the first fifty years of Christianity, but it is not as well preserved. One large section contains most of the second half of the book, with pieces missing. Smaller sections contain earlier parts of the book. Again, the similarity to the Masoretic is distinct.

3. What was at first considered to be the St. Mark's Lamech Scroll (because the name Lamech could be seen before the damaged scroll was opened) turned out to be a Genesis Apocryphon. It is in Aramaic and was probably written within fifty years before Christ. In places, it is Genesis verbatim, but in others it goes afield, such as in descriptions of Sara's beauty and of Abraham's journey through Canaan.

4. The St. Mark's Commentary on Habakkuk Scroll, written in Hebrew during the first fifty years of Christianity, is six inches wide and five feet long, but missing parts indicate it was originally several inches longer. The Book of Habakkuk has long been a point of difference among exegetes, mainly in terms of dating it. In it, God tells Habakkuk that He will send the Chaldeans (Babylonians) against the Jews as punishment for their wickedness. Since the Babylonians became the dominant power in this region around 600 B. C., Habakkuk, being a prophetic book, would have been written before that. However, some scholars have translated the Hebrew word form for "Chaldeans" as "Kittims"—Greeks, and the Greeks took over the region around 400 B. C., which reduces the age of the book.

77

As far as anybody knows, no "first" copy of any book of the Bible exists. Almost certainly, the Habakkuk Scroll is a copy of an earlier scroll, which, as yet, makes it impossible to determine when the commentary was first written. However, on the reference to the Chaldeans, the commentator says: "This refers to the Kittims (or Kittaeans), who are indeed swift and mighty in war, bent on destroying people far and wide and subduing them to their own domination." In a later reference to the prophesied invaders, he says: "Like a vulture they come from afar, from the isles of the sea, to devour all nations; and they are insatiable." Babylonia was an inland nation; the Greeks had islands, including Cyprus, once known as Kittim. This would seem to settle the matter but, as with much debate about the Bible, probably won't. Already it has been pointed out that the Jews usually referred to their enemies as Kittims or Kittaeans so that nobody would know whom they are talking about in case the document fell into the wrong hands.

One thing definitely settled is that the commentator was an Essene. He refers seven times to the "Teacher of Righteousness," which is sometimes translated "the teacher who expounds the Law aright." Other Dead Sea Scroll material establishes that the Teacher of Righteousness was once the head of the Qumran community and was killed by an unidentified "Wicked Priest."

5. One of the St. Mark's Scrolls has the title "Manual of Discipline," but Professor Sukenik and his son General Yadin have suggested "The Order of the Community." In two pieces, the scroll, as found, is six feet long and ten inches wide. However, in the Jordanian collection is a strip of the same coarse leather containing two columns of writing on the same subject, and it was definitely part of the same document. It is written in Hebrew, around 100 B. C.

The manuscript refers to a "Covenant of steadfast love," which is described as a community whose members are united in God. There is then a discussion of the two "spirits" in man—the Spirit of Light and Truth which exists in conflict with the Spirit of Darkness and Error. One is reminded of the Edgar Cayce concept of the Soul, seeking a return to God, in strife with the lingering

78

animal nature of the form it is occupying. The rest of the document sets forth the community's purpose, theology, communal life, probationary periods; and its legal, moral and liturgical practices, and it is quite similar to the information in Josephus about the Essenes.

The scroll is also remarkably similar to what has become known as the Damascus Document or Zadokite Document, which was found in the book repository of a medieval synagogue excavated in Egypt around 1878, and it was written in the Tenth Century A. D. Its two names evolve from the fact that it tells about a group of Jews who left Juda during a period of paganism and settled in Damascus and the priests with the group are called "sons of Zadok." Zadok was the priest who anointed David and was the High Priest of the Temple. Many of the rules and customs of this group are similar to the rules and customs described in the Manual of Discipline. The document also contains references to the Teacher of Righteousness and the Wicked Priest. Significantly, fragments of this document have been found in the Qumran caves, written much earlier. This has led some scholars to believe that there was a relationship between the two communities, even to the extent that they were the same group.

6. Another Hebrew University Scroll is titled: "The War of the Sons of Light and the Sons of Darkness." Written in Hebrew probably between 50 and 1 B. C., it is nine feet long and six inches wide and was found in its original linen wrapping. It consists of nineteen substantially preserved columns of text giving an elaborate description of an eschatological war to take place between the two factions, with God and His angels intervening to wipe out evil. General Yadin says that the strategem outlined in the document is definitely Roman, which could mean that the Roman technique had been observed and copied or that the plan was outlined by a Roman who had joined the community. The enemies are identified as the Kittims (or Kittaeans) of Egypt and Assyria. Both countries were traditional enemies of the Jews, but the reference to the Kittims could well mean the Greek or Roman dominators of Egypt and Assyria. Scholars point out that for two or three centuries before Christ and even

in the time of Christ many Jews were expecting the end of the world following a great war. Furthermore, this expectation is found in the contemporary literature of people of other lands. A similar idea is, for that matter, in Revelations. To some scholars, the scroll indicates that the war would last forty years and at the time of Divine intervention God would send the Messiah to lead to victory and then to rule a world of peace for the rest of time. Other scholars specify that the scroll is damaged at this point and that (1) the word form for "God" has been interpolated by others, that (2) the verb referring to the Messiah's appearance may be "begets" but is probably "is come," and that (3) the text is not clear on whether the Messiah would be of the entity of the Christus—thus the Second Coming in today's terms—or merely be a ruling king who was a good man and had been anointed by the High Priest when he took office. Contributing further to the uncertainty is the knowledge that the Essenes were a peaceful people who would not make weapons of war and who bore arms—a knife—only when they were traveling and felt they needed protection from robbers.

7. Also a Hebrew University Scroll are the Thanksgiving Psalms, so called because they usually begin with, "I thank you, O God. . . ." In Hebrew, the scroll was written within fifty years before Christianity. They were in four bundles when Sukenik acquired them, three of them crushed together and therefore separated into thirteen inch fragments in order to read them. There are eighteen psalms in all, similar to the Old Testament but not of equal poetic beauty, and some of them are believed to have been written by the Teacher of Righteousness, who remains a man of mystery.

The debate among the scholars on the real identity of the Teacher of Righteousness and the Wicked Priest present the mere student with a chaotic confusion of possibilities. Until the scholars decide, it is enough to acknowledge that both men did exist at one time · and at the same time, one being a holy man, the other obviously not so holy. That the Teacher of Righteousness was a priest, maybe a High Priest, is indicated both in the Qumran scrolls and the Damascus Document. It appears that he might at one time have been a man of great authority in the land, and he was either forced out of power or decided to give up power in order to get away from the evil surrounding it. If he lived in the Second Century B. C., as some evidence suggests, he probably supervised the construction of the Qumran monastery or house of studies. There is evidence that the building was erected around 150 B. C., give or take several years, and was destroyed around A. D. 68, the evidence being in the form of coins and artifacts found during the excavation. If the Teacher lived in the First Century B. C., and some evidence supports this, then the house of studies was already there and was being used for purposes which the Teacher approved or he would have gone somewhere else. Other evidence indicates that the structure was not occupied for a period of thirty years, beginning in 31 B. C. It is known that an earthquake shook this area that year, which may be why the people went away. The fact that they returned on the eve of Christianity may be significant.

The likelihood for the earlier existence of the Teacher is supported by the fact that the Manual of Discipline Scroll, written around 100 B. C., refers to him in the past tense. He was dead. According to the documents, the Teacher could foretell the future, which made him a prophet. The Sadducees, who accepted as Law only the Pentateuch, rejected the writings of the prophets and prophets themselves. For three hundred years before Christ, anyone who claimed to be a prophet faced execution during a Sadduccee reign. It is probable, then, that it was a Sadducean High Priest who brought about the death of the Teacher, by crucifixion. This was a Roman, not Jewish, form of execution, which leads some scholars to believe that the death might have taken place at a later date.

The Teacher foretold his death, even the form of it, and he also foretold that he would return. The Qumran literature suggests that the Teacher's return would be preceded by the return of Elijah or the "son" of Elijah. Throughout the writings, there is a strong Messianic anticipation, sometimes in association with the death of the Teacher, and this had led some scholars to deduce that the brotherhood at Qumran believed that its resurrected (reincarnated?) Teacher would be the Messiah. Both the Manual of Discipline and the Damascus Document refer to another manuscript with the word-form title of "HGW." Nobody can figure out what that means because there are no vowel indications. But both documents say, in effect, "All that is not delineated here can be found in HGW." In view of the many gaps in the Qumran picture and of all the guesswork resulting from them, this makes "HGW" a tremendously important document. It is puzzling, therefore, that not a scrap of it has been found. Was there just one copy of it at Qumran? Was it found in a cave by some early Bedouin who then lost it or destroyed it? It is known that certain sacred writings existed at this time that were of such mystical scope that they could be read only by those specially trained because their contents might shatter the faith of lesser men. Sometimes such books were even destroyed to put them out of circulation. Was "HGW" such a book? Shall we ever know?

FIVE

The Edgar Cayce Life Readings contain many references to Mount Carmel, the mountain where Elijah challenged the priests of Baal and triumphed over them. Elijah lived on the mountain before and after this event; so did Elisha, his successor. Also residing on the mountain with Elisha and after him were a number of men who were called "sons of Elijah," and their community was considered both a school of the prophets and a school for the prophets. Carmel has always been regarded as a holy mountain. In the middle of the Second Millennium B. C., the geographical lists at Karnak, the governing seat of pharoahs, called Carmel "the sacred cape." Iamblichus, the Fourth Century B. C. Syrian philosopher, wrote that Carmel was "the most holy of all mountains and forbidden of access to many." Around A. D. 100, Tacitus, the Roman historian, reported that Vespasian, while leading the war against the Jews some forty years previous, had offered sacrifices on Elijah's open-air altar and thereupon received an oracle indicating that he would become the next Roman emperor, which he did. Tradition locates the altar on the rocky plateau of el-Muhraqa on the southeast flank of the range.

These days, the suburbs of the Israeli port city of Haifa rise on the face of the mountain that looks to the sea. Atop the mountain are a church and a Carmelite monastery that can be seen for miles at sea. Rising to eighteen hundred feet, Carmel extends southeastward some fifteen miles. Its Hebrew name—*karmel*—means orchard, but here suggests a pleasant woodland. The long mountain is still heavily wooded, but mostly with scrub growth. The Bible remarks on the magnificent forest that was once here in a place blessed by God. Mount Carmel, too, has become involved in the mystery of the Essenes.

Nobody knows for certain whether the Sons of the Prophet remained on Mount Carmel after the departure of Elijah and the subsequent death of Elisha, which was around 800 B. C. On the other hand, nobody knows whether they went away. Two hundred years later, the Prophet Micah admonishes: "Feed thy people with thy rod, the flock of thine heritage, which dwell solitarily in the wood in the midst of Carmel." So somebody was there. And two hundred years after that, Malachi, the last of the prophets, finishes his testimony by quoting God as saying: "Behold, I will send you Elijah the prophet before the coming of the great and dreadful day of the Lord. And he shall turn the heart of the fathers to the children and the heart of the children to their fathers, lest I come and smite the earth with a curse."

Though the Sadducean threat discouraged prophets for the three centuries before Jesus, the final words of Malachi stirred a devotion to Elijah among devout Jews, almost to the extent of a cult. People made pilgrimages to the altar on the mountain and offered sacrifices in the prophet's name, believing that he was waiting somewhere in the heavens for the moment when God would send him back with the good news that the Messiah was on the way. Whether the Messiah would be "priestly," of the lineage of Aaron, or "kingly," of the lineage of Israel, no one was sure. The Manual of Discipline Scroll suggests that perhaps more than one Messiah was expected in "the coming of a prophet and the Anointed Ones of Aaron and Israel." The Damascus Document, on the other hand, speaks of "the Anointed One of Aaron and Israel." Whether there was a change in opinion or just an error in recopying cannot now be determined.

In any event, the anticipation of Elijah before the arrival of the Messiah was such a strongly held view that when John the Baptist began his mission of baptizing and telling people to "make straight the way of the Lord," the priests and Levites themselves went to him and asked if he was Elijah. He said no, but Jesus later said of him: "And if you are willing to receive it, he was Elijah who was to come." Even today, exegetes cannot agree whether John was Elijah or just a symbol of Elijah or whether Elijah has yet to return for the announcement of the Second Coming.

Tradition suggests that Christian monasticism began in Egypt in the Fourth Century A. D., but there is every reason to believe that it could have started much earlier and much closer to where Christianity began. Monasticism itself goes far back into history, in India and Asia Minor; and it is now acknowledged that certain members of the Essenes were monks, in that they took vows. Also, the hermit life goes far back. Ancient caves found on Mount Carmel are clearly too small for anything but single occupancy, and the number of them found indicates that, at one time or from time to time, men—monks, perhaps—chose to live the eremitical life in this holy place. There is some evidence to support this.

In A. D. 330, the Roman Emperor Constantine I moved his capital from Rome to the ancient city of Byzantium, in what is now Turkey, and changed its name to Constantinople. By this time the Christian Church had taken on an organizational structure, under the supervision of the Bishop of Rome, an office first held by Simon Peter. Constantine, a convert to Christianity, considered himself to be both the head of the state and the head of the Church; and when he moved his state to Constantinople, he expected the Church to move with him. The Bishop—then Pope Sylvester I—refused to go, feeling that the Church should stay in Rome where, as a church, it got started. Subsequent popes and the heirs of Constantine continued to argue about this, until the Emperor announced that the Patriarch of Constantinople would be the ruler of the Church in the East, thus producing a schism. The church at Constantinople became the Eastern Orthodox Church, sometimes called the Byzantine Church.

The Fall of Jerusalem to the Romans in A. D. 70 was accompanied by a thorough destruction of the country, followed by a long period of desolation. Destruction came again early in the Seventh Century with the spread of Islam from Arabia westward across Africa into Spain and northward into Asia Minor to Turkey and into Eastern Europe. Despite the Moslem domination of the country, Christians of both the East and West were allowed to visit their holy places, to build churches and shrines, and to practice their faith, and this went on for almost two hundred years. Then the Moslem power passed from Arabia to Turkey, where the religious division in Europe had become political as well. Now the Western—Latin—Christians were persecuted along with the Jews, and the Holy Land was closed to them. Out of this grew the Crusades, and for the next two hundred years the land of the Jews was again torn by war, with power over the country changing hands continually.

Among the Crusaders who arrived around 1150 was one Berthold, a Frenchman and a Latin priest. He was at Antioch when the town was attacked and, during his prayers for victory, he was Divinely informed that the attack was being allowed as punishment for the Crusaders who had forgotten their holy mission and had turned to looting, plundering and carousing. Berthold offered himself as a sacrifice, promising that if the Christians were allowed to win he would spend the rest of his life in service to the Virgin. He had a vision in which Jesus, the Virgin and Simon Peter appeared, a great

85

cross of light glowing behind them, and Jesus told him that the Crusaders would first have to give up their evil ways before they would be given the power to win the battle. Berthold went among the Crusaders, exhorting them to change their lives. They did and they won the battle. Now Berthold was ready to fulfill his promise.

Tradition holds that the Prophet Elijah had a vision in which he saw the future mother of Jesus, and for this reason he held a place of honor among the first Christians. Tradition also holds that the vision occurred on Mount Carmel, and for this reason the first Christians made pilgrimages to the mountain, honoring both Elijah and the Virgin. Knowing this and knowing that the mountain was near, Berthold decided to go there for a period of prayer and meditation, during which he hoped God would reveal to him how he was to carry out his promise of lifelong service. When he got there and located the remains of Elijah's altar, he was surprised to find, as well, a small monastery housing a number of Byzantine priests. They told him that their predecessors had been attending the shrine for generations and that, centuries back, when the first priests arrived they found the site occupied by a community of Jewish Christians who were conducting a house of studies. These Christians told the Byzantines that they were the spiritual heirs of a Jewish monastic group which had lived and studied there before the birth of Jesus. Since it is now known that the only Jewish sect which led anything resembling the monastic life were the Essenes, it can be presumed that the earlier Jews were Essenes. And the Christians told the Byzantines that the settlement could trace its history back to the days of Elijah and his School of the Prophets.

In all likelihood, the meeting between the Jewish Christians and the Byzantines took place before the break between Rome and Constantinople, and thus the two groups were able to join their spiritual efforts in a single liturgy. After the break, certain changes were made in the Eastern liturgy. Evidently these changes were accepted by the settlement on the mountain or else were gradually introduced by Eastern priests who, over the years, arrived from Byzantium to join the community.

In any event, the Eastern rites were being practiced by the monks when Berthold got there.

There is no record of events which led Berthold to decide that he was to carry out his promise by living an eremitical life there on Mount Carmel. There is no record to identify others who joined him. There is no record to establish whether the Byzantines joined Berthold's group, as the earlier Byzantines had joined with the Jewish Christians. But there are records of other things.

It is believed that Berthold died in 1195, and he was succeeded as head of his group by one Brocard or Burchard, also a Frenchman. Between 1205 and 1210, Brocard approached Albert, the Latin Patriarch of Jerusalem and an Italian, to write a constitution which would serve as the rules for the community then identified as the Brothers of the Blessed Virgin Mary of Mount Carmel. The community became better known as the Carmelites. Albert's constitution required the members to live alone in separate cells or caves, to meet daily for Mass, to recite the psalms together at specified hours (Daily Office), to work with their hands, to observe poverty, perpetual abstinence and long silences, and to be obedient to their prior. Since the constitution was written by the Latin Patriarch, it follows that the liturgy on Mount Carmel, at least among the Carmelites, was Roman.

As such, the Carmelites needed the approval of Rome to exist as a religious community within the Church. The constitution reached Rome in 1226, by which time numerous other monastic orders were springing up everywhere, and, to curtail the development, Pope Honorious III decided to suppress the Carmelites, among others. But the Virgin appeared to him and told him to approve the Order, so he did.

Meanwhile, the fighting continued in the Holy Land, with power changing hands again and again. By 1238, life had become too risky at Mount Carmel and groups of Carmelites began moving out, establishing centers elsewhere, at Cyprus, Sicily, France and England. All of them flourished, and within ten years the Carmelites had over one hundred fifty houses throughout Europe, all of them considering themselves to be distinctly affiliated with

Mount Carmel. Prefixed to the Carmelite constitution in 1281 was this statement: "From the times when the prophets Elias and Eliseus (Catholic spelling) dwelt devoutly on Mount Carmel, holy fathers both of the old and new testament . . . lived praiseworthy lives in holy penitence by the fountain of Elias in a holy succession uninterruptedly maintained." The statement makes the Carmelite conviction of direct lineage to Elijah quite clear. Moreover, when statues of the early leaders of the Carmelites were placed in the Vatican, a statue of Elijah was included, identified: "Founder of the Carmelite Order."

In 1291, the Turks again swept across the Holy Land, conquering the port city of Acre, and with that the efforts of the Crusaders were definitely put to an end. Christians—West or East—had to get out of the country or die. The Carmelites left and their establishment on the mountain was destroyed. Even so, the popularity of the Order in Europe continued to grow, and communities for women were begun. With the growth came a relaxation of the rules, which was displeasing to some of the members. For example, some rich person would give the Carmelites a house in a city, and they would move into it. In the city, they could not support themselves by working with their hands, by farming, so they turned to other means of support—hospitals, schools, orphanages. In such areas of work, they could not maintain their rule of long silences, so the rule was modified. Unable to farm, they could not obtain enough vegetables to adhere to their original rule against eating meat, so the rule was modified to allow meat three times a week. Working in cities in winter, they could not go about the snowy, muddy streets in their traditional sandals without the risk of becoming ill, so the rule was modified to let them wear shoes. And, being more active, they had less time for the hours of mental prayer and meditation which had originally been specified for them. As minor as some of these things may seem, they were of critical importance to members of the Order who felt the Carmelites were drifting a long way from their true purpose of spiritual service above the temporal.

Reform was brought about in the sixteenth century by

two spiritual giants. One became known as St. Teresa of Avila, the other St. John of the Cross. Both were acknowledged mystics in their own lifetimes; both underwent a staggering horizon of supernatural experiences. Both were Carmelites, both wanting the Order to return to its stricter observances. Despite severe opposition from most of their Carmelite superiors, they obtained permission from bishops to open isolated monasteries where men or women could adhere to the earlier rules. At first they were called Contemplative Carmelites; then, because they resumed the custom of wearing sandals instead of shoes, they became known as the Discalced Carmelites, *calceatus* being the Latin word for shoe.

As the movement grew stronger, so did the disagreement among the Carmelite leadership. It eventually became necessary for King Philip II of Spain to intervene, using his influence at Rome to allow the Discalced Carmelites to be set up as a separate province within the Carmelite Order. Finally, in 1593, Pope Clement VIII established the Discalced Carmelites as an independent religious order with their own superior general and administration.

In 1634 a group of Discalced Carmelites traveled to Palestine and reoccupied Mount Carmel, returning, in effect, to their birthplace which they had not inhabited since their expulsion in 1291. At the same time, both branches of the Carmelites found themselves involved in another conflict. There had come into being in Belgium a group of Jesuit scholars whose task it was to sift through the massive Church literature that had accumulated and try to separate the facts from the fictions. They became known as the Bollandists, this from John Bolland, the second Jesuit to head the work and to supervise most of it. When the Bollandists came upon the Carmelite claim that their Order had been founded by Elijah they said this simply was not true because it was not possible. The fact, they said, that there had evidently been a succession of monastic communities on Mount Carmel from Elijah's School of the Prophets to Berthold's Carmelites did not suggest a specific lineage as to origin. The Carmelites argued that their claim of specific succession was as valid as the claim of specific succession of the popes from

Peter. The debate grew fierce; low blows were struck by both sides. In 1698, Pope Innocent XII ordered both sides to shut up and never to discuss the subject again.

The monastery which the returning Discalced Carmelites built was destroyed twice by Turks: in 1720 and 1831. The present monastery was finished in 1853, and it houses the international school of philosophy for the Order. The superior general, who resides in Rome, is, according to the Order's constitution, the prior of the Mount Carmel monastery.

Excavations in 1958 uncovered what is accepted to be Elijah's altar, the cave where he lived, the fountain of Elijah, and the remnants of an ancient monastery. The City of Haifa has since appropriated funds for further exploration of the mountain, but because of the continuing Israeli-Arab War, the work has not begun. Thus the magnificent mountain still holds its many secrets.

The King James version of the Bible contains the word "Carmelite" four times, all in the books of Samuel. Three of the references are to "Nabal the Carmelite" and one to "Hezrai the Carmelite." Both the Douay Bible and The New English Bible translate the expression as "of Carmel." But King James was the Bible Cayce knew and loved, so he was acquainted with the reference as "Carmelite." But the only time he used the word during readings he did so in an entirely different context.

On February 19, 1941, Cayce did the fifth Life Reading on a fifty-year-old woman identified as Entity 993, and he gave her information about an earlier incarnation during the time of Jesus. He told her that her father, Archaus by name, was a close adherent of the Essenic school of thought regarding religion, and Cayce said: "The entity had the greater teachings, or was acquainted with the greater teachings, of the Carmelites—now the Essenes." By "now," Cayce meant *then*.

In 1941, not even the Carmelites themselves were associating the Order with the Essenes, though some of them now do. In 1941, nothing new had been learned about the Essenes since Josephus; and though Josephus did say there were Essenic communities throughout the land, he made no reference to Mount Carmel as an

Essenic headquarters. Furthermore, there was little likelihood that in 1941 Edgar Cayce knew much, if anything, about the Carmelites. The first Carmelite monastery in America was established near Milwaukee, Wisconsin, in 1906, an event which would scarcely come to the attention of the young photographer who was trying to earn a living in a small Southern town. Once again, the student must rely on the experience of the surviving person closest to Cayce—his son Hugh Lynn—for affirmation of the fact that the man had no conscious knowledge of Carmelites, with or without shoes, and had not in any other reading referred to them in the same context, as a religious group which inhabited Mount Carmel. On the other hand, Cayce had by this time referred to Essenes at Mount Carmel in many readings over several years. During Edgar Cayce's life time, the basic interest in his information about Essenes was their influence on the life of Jesus Christ, and Cayce was able to provide many fascinating details. It wasn't until after the discovery of the Dead Sea Scrolls and subsequent writings about them that Hugh Lynn Cayce and members of the Association for Research and Enlightenment intensified their studies of the readings for more specifics about Mount Carmel. Since it had been established without doubt that the Essenes did indeed have a community at the Dead Sea, as Edgar Cayce had, in effect, predicted, then, in view of the readings, any evidence of Essenes at Mount Carmel would serve as further substantiation of Cayce's subconscious contact with things past. In 1965, Hugh Lynn Cayce and several A. R. E. members made a special trip to Israel in quest of some evidence, and they had good reason.

In 1952, a copper scroll had been found in Cave Three at Qumran. It had originally been one long strip of copper, but at some point it was cut into two, the two parts rolled together and placed in a jar. Passing centuries had caused the two pieces to oxidize, one to the other, and when the scroll was found it could not be unrolled without the risk of damaging the lettering. Four years later, scientists at the University of Manchester, England, solved the problem. Plastic substances were sprayed in the space between the two sheets of copper and the scrolls were then "baked." Thus hardened, layer by layer could be sawed off, cleaned and photographed. In this way, ninety-five per cent of the text was recovered, and the text was bewildering.

Written around the middle of the First Christian Century, the scroll is a blend of formal and informal Hebrew writing, and there are errors in spelling and grammar. The text is, in effect, a treasure map, and the treasure is enormous. But the clues are so vague that the experts suggest that the treasure will never be found—if indeed it ever existed. Here are some samples:

"In the large cistern which is in the Court of the Peristyle, in a recess at the bottom of it, hidden in a hole opposite the upper opening: 900 talents."

"In the cistern which is below the rampart, on the east side, in a place hollowed out of the rock: 600 bars of silver."

"Close by, below the southern corner of the portico, at Zadok's tomb, underneath the pilaster in the exedra: a vessel of incense in pine wood and a vessel of incense in cassia wood."

"In the pit nearby, toward the north in a hole opening toward the north near the graves, there is a copy of this document with explanations, measurements and all details."

In all, over two hundred tons of gold and silver are listed, plus other items of value, and the question puzzling the experts is: How could such a fantastic treasure ever be accumulated in the first place? Some of the experts are convinced there never was such a treasure, that the scroll was written as a prank—a joke. If so, then somebody certainly put in an awful lot of work just for laughs. Some experts feel the document is a product of the Zealots, a militant, warlike sect that strongly resisted the Roman occupation. Josephus reports that in A. D. 66 bands of Zealots overran the royal palaces and a Roman headquarters and made off with every valuable they could carry. At the time, the Zealots also had access to the Temple in Jerusalem, with all its treasures. These experts surmise that, on realizing that the Romans were about to conquer the city, the Zealots hid the valuables in a variety of places and prepared the scroll for future use in recovering them. If so, what was the scroll doing in a cave so near an Essene community? Though the Essenes expected an ultimate war against the Sons of Darkness, they were a peaceful people, hardly likely to be friendly enough with the Zealots to be trusted with such an important document, no matter how vaguely it was written.

The fact that the scroll is copper seems to indicate an intention for durability. Holes along the edges of the scroll have led some scholars to conclude that it was once nailed to a wall, which would have been a strange thing to do with a document so secretive in tone. It could just as well have been nailed to a wooden table while being worked on. The two different kinds of writing, one like printing and the other like script, plus the errors in spelling and grammar, suggest to some that the document was/ quickly prepared, perhaps under the pressure of danger, and this may be. But the reference to the more detailed document about the hidden treasure may suggest that the other document was written with more care and less pressure. The copper scroll refers to graves, and there is a cemetery at Qumran, but the fact that the scroll is copper, and is the only copper scroll found at Qumran, raises the possibility that it may have been written somewhere else. Information derived from the Edgar Cayce readings supports the probability that though Qumran was an important Essenic community it was not the actual headquarters of the sect. The readings, at least in terms of important events, put the headquarters at Mount Carmel. It is a possibility, therefore, that the treasure listed in the scroll had actually accumulated at Mount Carmel. Generation after generation, people joined the sect, and, following the rule, donated their possessions to the common fund, for the common good and for sake of equality for all. This being so, the treasure would not be at Qumran or Jerusalem but there on the mountain at the sea.

Hugh Lynn Cayce and his friends spent three weeks at Mount Carmel, searching for evidence of a treasure that was quite different. The Edgar Cayce readings had described a temple of some size on the eastern face of the mountain. That it should be on the eastern face was in keeping with information later acquired from the Dead

Sea Scrolls: the Essenes at Qumran conducted a religious service every morning during the rising of the sun. This has led some observers to the conclusion that the Essenes were sun worshipers, though this seems a remote likelihood for a group of monotheistic and devout Jews who were, according to the Cayce readings, well aware of their role in the birth and training of Jesus. If, for that matter, the sun itself were the decisive factor, then the Carmelites now living on the mountain are also sun-worshipers: the seven canonical hours of the Divine Office, prayers derived from the Psalms, requires them to recite Matins, the first hour, at dawn.

It was important for Hugh Lynn Cayce and his companions to find some evidence of the remains of the Mount Carmel temple in order to give some substance to information which had resulted from what must have been an extremely stirring Edgar Cayce reading. The reading was held on June 27, 1937, beginning at four-fifteen in the afternoon, in the Cayce home at Virginia Beach. Gertrude Cayce conducted the reading. Gladys Davis was there, taking notes. Hugh Lynn was there. Also there was Thomas Sugrue, a Catholic, a writer, an editor, and later Cayce's biographer in *There Is A River*. After Cayce had fallen asleep, his wife began the reading with:

"You will have before you the entity Thomas Sugrue, present in this room. You will now continue with the information on the life and history of the Master, beginning now with detailed information on the group which was preparing for the coming of the Christ, giving the name of group, names of members who figured prominently in the active preparation; relating the signs, symbols and visions which indicated to this group that the time was at hand. You will then answer the questions that may be asked."

Cayce seemed to nod. He said: "Yes, we have the entity here, Thomas Sugrue, with the desire and the purpose for the understanding and knowledge of the physical experience of the Master's in the earth." Cayce moved a bit, as though making himself comfortable. He said:

"In those days, when there had been more and more of the leaders of the people in Carmel—the original

94

place where the School of Prophets was established during Elijah's time, Samuel's, these were called then Essenes. Théy were students of what you would call astrology, numerology, phrenology, and those phases of that study of the return of individuals—or incarnation. These studies were then the reasons that there had been a proclaiming that certain 'periods' were a cycle; and these had been the studies then of Arestole, Enos, Mathias, Judas, and those that were in the care or supervision of the 'school' —as you would term. These had been persecuted by other leaders, the cause being in the interpretation of 'Sadducees'—or 'There is no resurrection' or 'There is no incarnation,' which is what it meant in those periods.

"In the lead of these were those who had been chosen because of the positions of the stars that stand, as it were, in the dividing of the ways between the 'universal,' which is the common vision of the solar system of the sun, and those without the spheres or, by its common name, the North Star, because its variation made for those cycles that would be incoordinant with those choices of leadership that had been determined by others, at the beginning of the preparation, for the three hundred years in this period. Those in charge at the time were Mathias, Enos, Judas.

"In these signs, then, was the new cycle, which was then—as we have in the astrological—the beginning of the Piscean Age, or that position of the Polar Star or North Star as related to the southern clouds. These made for the signs, these made for the symbols, the sign to be used and the manner of the sign's approach and the like. These, then, were the beginnings, and these were the matters that made a part of the studies during that period.

"Then there were, again, those soundings—that is, the approach of that which had been handed down and had been the experiences from the sages of old: that an angel was to speak. Because this occurred when there was the choosing of the mate who had—in the belief of those so close—been immaculately conceived, this brought to the focal point the preparation of the mother.

"Then when there were those periods when there was the dumbness to the priest and he, Zacharias, was slain for his repeating of same in the hearing of those of his own school, this made for those fears that made the necessary preparations for the wedding, the preparations for the birth and the preparations for those activities for the preservation (physically) of the child—or the flight into Egypt.

"Ready for questions."

Gertrude Cayce glanced at Tom Sugrue and nodded. Sugrue moved to the edge of his seat. He asked: "Is the teaching of the Roman Catholic Church—that Mary was without original sin from the moment of her conception in the womb of Ann—correct?"

Cayce sounded impatient. "It would be correct in *any* case. Correct more in this. Because, as for the material teachings of that just referred to, you see: From the beginning, Mary was the twin-soul of the Master in the first entrance into the earth!"

"Was Ann prepared for her part in the drama as mother of Mary?"

"Only as in the general," Cayce said, "not as specific as Mary, after Mary being pointed out. See, there was no belief in the fact that Ann proclaimed, that the child was without father. It's like proclaiming today that the Master was immaculately conceived—many people say: 'Impossible!' They said that it isn't in compliance with the natural law. It IS a natural law, as has been indicated by the projection of 'mind' into matter and thus making itself a separation to become encased in matter, as happened with man. That there has been an encasement was the beginning. Then there must be an end when this must be—or may be—broken, and this began at that particular period, though not the only, and this particular period with Ann and then the Master *as* the son but the *only* begotten of the Father in the flesh *as* a son *of* an immaculately conceived daughter."

Sugrue asked: "Neither Mary nor Jesus, then, had a human father?"

"Neither Mary nor Jesus had a human father," Cayce said simply. "There were one *soul,* so far as the earth is concerned, because otherwise she would not be incarnated in flesh, you see."

"How were the maidens selected and by whom?"

"By all of those who chose to give children that were

96

perfect in body and in mind for the service in the Essenes," said Cayce. "Ann—or Anna—gave Mary; and in the presentation, she could not be refused because of the perfectness of Mary's body. However, many people questioned Ann's claim that she conceived without knowing a man, and this produced a division. The other maidens were chosen as a representative of the 'twelve' in the various phases that had been—or that made up —Israel, or man."

"How old was Mary at the time she was chosen?"

"Four, when chosen for the Essenes; between twelve and thirteen when she was designated as the one chosen by the angel on the stair."

Sugrue asked Cayce to describe the training and preparation of this group of twelve girls among whom, the Essenes believed, was the one who would become the mother of the Christus, now that the hour had come, and Cayce said: "Trained as to physical exercise first; then trained as to mental exercises, as related to chastity, purity, love, patience, endurance—rigorously, by what would be termed by many in the present as persecutions but actually as tests for physical and mental strength. This was done under the supervision of those that cared for the nourishments by the protection in the food values. These were the manners and the way they were trained, directed, protected."

"Were they put on special diet?"

"No wine, no fermented drink ever given. Special foods, yes. These were kept balanced according to that which had been first set by Aran and Rata."

"In what manner was Joseph informed of his part in the birth of Jesus?"

"First by Mathias or Judah. Then as this did not coincide with his own feelings, next in a dream and then the direct voice. And whenever the voice, this always is accompanied by odors as well as lights. And oft the description of the lights is the vision, see?"

Sugrue wondered: "Why was he disturbed when Mary became with child while yet a virgin?"

"Because of his natural surroundings and because of his advanced age to that of the virgin when she was given," said Cayce. "He was disturbed because of what people might say. Yet when assured, you see, that this was the divine, assured not only by his brethren but by the voice and by these experiences, then he knew. For, you see, there was from the time of the first promise—while she was still yet in training after the choice, there was a period of some three to four years. Yet when he went to claim her as the bride, at the period of—or—between sixteen and seventeen, she was found with child."

"How old was Joseph at the time of the marriage?"

"Thirty-six."

"How old was Mary at the time of the marriage?"

"Sixteen."

"At what time after the birth of Jesus did Mary and Joseph take up the normal life of a married couple and bring forth the issue called James?"

"Ten years. Then they came in succession: James, the daughter, Jude."

Cayce was asked for a description of the choosing of Mary, and he said: "It took place on the temple steps —or those that led to the altar; these were called the temple steps. These were those upon which the sun shone as it arose of a morning, when there were the first periods of the chosen maidens going to the altar for prayer, as well as for the burning of the incense. On this day, as they mounted the steps, all were bathed in the morning sun, which not only made a beautiful picture but clothed all as in purple and gold. As Mary reached the top step, then, then there was the thunder and lightning, and the angel led the way, taking the child by the hand, before the altar. This was the manner of choice; this was the showing of the way, for she led the others on *this* particular day."

"Was this the orthodox Jewish temple or the Essene temple?"

"The Essene temple, to be sure. Because of the adherence to those visions as proclaimed by Zacharias in the orthodox temple, he (Zacharias) was slain even with his hands upon the thorns of the altar. Hence those as were being protected were in Carmel, while Zacharias was in the temple of Jerusalem."

"Was Mary required to wait ten years before knowing Joseph?"

98

"Only, you see, until Jesus went to be taught by others did the normal or natural associations come—but not required. It was a choice of them both because of their own feelings. But when He was from without the roof and under the protection of those who were the guides (that is, the priests), these associations began then as normal experiences."

"Were the parents of John the Messenger members of the band which prepared Jesus?"

"As has just been indicated, Zacharias at first was a member of what you would term the orthodox priesthood. Mary and Elizabeth were members of the Essenes, you see; and for this very reason Zacharias kept Elizabeth in the mountains and in the hills. Yet when there was the announcing of the birth and Zacharias proclaimed his belief, the murder, the death took place."

"Where was the wedding performed, of Mary and Joseph?"

"In the temple there at Carmel."

"Where did the couple live during the pregnancy?"

"Mary spent the most of the time in the hills of Judea, a portion of the time with Joseph in Nazareth. From there they went to Bethany to be taxed—or to register, as ye would term."

"Who assisted as midwife?"

Referring to earlier readings, Cayce said: "This has been touched up through these sources. And as the daughter of the innkeeper and those about assisted and aided, these have seen the glory, much, in their experiences."

"Do we celebrate Christmas at approximately the right time?"

"Not a great variation, for there having been the many changes in the accounting of time or accounting for the periods from the various times when time is counted. Not far wrong—the twenty-fourth, twenty-fifth of December, as ye have your time now."

"Who were the parents of Joseph?"

"That as recorded by Matthew, as is given, you see; one side recorded by Matthew, the other by Luke—these on various sides but of the house of David, as was also Mary of the house of David."

"Were Mary and Joseph known to each other socially before the choosing for them to be man and wife?"

"As would be chosen in a lodge, not as ye would term by visitations, nor as chosen by the sect of the families. In those periods, in most of the Jewish families, the arrangements were made by the parents of the contracting parties, you see; while in this—these were not as contracting parties from their families. For Ann and her daughter were questioned as to belonging to *any*, you see. Then it was not a choice altogether, as that they were appointed by the leaders of the sect or of the group or of the lodge or of the church, for this is the church that is called the Catholic now, and is the closest. These were kept, then, in that way of choice between them, and choice as pointed out by the divine forces. We are through for the present."

Hugh Lynn Cayce and his friends went to Israel in hopes of finding some evidence, even the slightest shred of evidence, that an Essene community of some kind once existed on the eastern slopes of Mount Carmel. They realized that their chances were slim. They had, in the first place, allotted themselves just three weeks, scarcely enough time for an in-depth investigation, and none of them had sufficient foundation in archaeology to achieve much in that area. But they knew the Edgar Cayce readings well, so if they came upon anything, any evidence, any information, which in any way reflected something which had been said in the readings, they would have been satisfied. Moreover, if it could be established that even one item listed on the copper scroll at Qumran had been found at Mount Carmel, they would have been more than satisfied that the Essenes had been here.

They were satisfied, but in a different way. They visited the cave of Elijah. They saw the fountain—spring, actually—of Elijah. They inspected the ruins of an ancient Carmelite monastery. They stood before what is accepted as the remnants of Elijah's altar. They walked the eastern face of the mountain. They found some pottery, pieces of glass, shards, all of some age but not old enough; Hugh Lynn Cayce found an ancient coin, and they entered some caves which evidently had once been inhabited, though nothing of value was in them now. Even so, there was satisfaction in the experience. To be at last on this holy mountain, where men and women of both the Old and New Testaments had lived, to walk its paths, to breathe its air, to enter its caves, so silent with secrets of the past, was in itself a spiritual treasure, and each man in the group felt profoundly stirred by the adventure.

They talked to people. From a Carmelite monk, one Father Elias, coincidentally enough, they heard for the first time the Carmelite version of the origin of the Order, with Elijah. Father Elias was willing to concede that perhaps there had once been an Essene community on the mountain, that the Jewish Christians who had been there when the Byzantines arrived were, perhaps, heirs by a few generations of Essenes, but he would not be certain. As a Carmelite still subject to the papal edict for silence on this matter, he could not.

From Dr. J. Elgavish, director of the Haifa Museum of Fine Arts, they learned that next to no archaeological excavations had been conducted on Mount Carmel. Some money for an expedition had been appropriated by the city, but not enough, and the times were too uncertain to try anything. They learned, too, that over the centuries it had been the custom of builders to use ruins as quarries and that if any of the treasures listed on the copper scrolls had ever been on the mountain, they had in all likelihood been found and taken away by now.

Then something unusual happened. Being the type of men they were, Hugh Lynn Cayce and his friends, men of different faiths, began their day with prayer and meditation, and they knew from experience that during these moments significant thoughts or ideas could occur. One of them, who, for now, prefers to be nameless, was deep in meditative thought one morning when in his mind's eye he saw a man about fifty, dressed in Biblical or monastic garb. He was wearing a dark robe with a hood and a golden cord. He was walking with a bow-legged gait toward a wall and climbed up to the third rung of a five-rung ladder and proceeded to put an object into a chamber in the wall.

Later that same morning, the group visited the ancient monastery. Something about the place gave this man the

101

feeling of having been there before, and the sensation grew stronger when he saw, propped against a wall, a ladder similiar to the one he had seen in meditation, except that it was double the length. As though directed, this man wandered away from the others and came to an old part of the ruins. He closed his eyes, waiting. Then, hearing a sound behind him, he turned and saw standing there the same hooded figure, who said to him: "Go down to the steps and meditate there on the third step." The man in the robe then disappeared.

This man looked about and saw at last some steps, hidden by the weeds and bushes, some steps leading down the wadi. So he went down to the third step and he sat down and he closed his eyes again. After some moments, these words entered his mind: "What you are looking for is not here."

SIX

The Essenes quite clearly expected the Messiah to arise within their ranks. Moreover, they expected the Messiah soon. Evidently they expected Him to be a layman, thus a kingly Messiah, of the house of David. The evidence for this is in the Manual of Discipline, in the portions dealing with the protocol for meals. Always it is the priest who blesses the bread and must (grape juice) and is the first to partake of them. Even during the Messianic Banquet, when the Messiah would be present, the priest still gives the blessing and takes the first servings. Then the Messiah. Then the others. This protocol has led some scholars to surmise that although the Essenes expected the Messiah to be of mighty stature politically they did not look to Him for spiritual leadership. These scholars point out that Dead Sea Scrolls and fragments written during the First Christian Century do not suggest that the Messiah had arrived and that He was Jesus, and, furthermore, that the Christian writings of this period make no mention of the Essenes.

Josephus, who wrote extensively on the Essenes, had this to say about Jesus in his history of the Jews:

"Now there was about this time Jesus, a wise man, if it be lawful to call him a man, for he was a doer of many wonderful works—a teacher of such men as receive the truth with pleasure. He drew over to him both many of the Jews and many of the Gentiles. He was (the) Christ; and when Pilate, at the suggestion of the principal men amongst us, had condemned him to the cross, those that loved him at the first did not forsake him, for he appeared to them alive again the third day, as the divine prophets had foretold these and ten thousand other wonderful things concerning him; and the tribe of Christians, so named from him, are not extinct at this day."

One problem in the debate currently raging among scholars on the relationships of the Bible, the Dead Sea literature and the origins of Christianity is that some scholars seem to think that the information is now all in. It isn't. The Qumran literature refers to documents which have not been found, and may never be. Certainly there are many other ancient documents which would answer a lot of questions if they could ever be found. Because the Qumran literature contains no references to Jesus doesn't mean He and the sect never made contact. Because the New Testament contains no references to the Essenes doesn't mean the first Christians had no contact with the sect. If actual documentation for such contacts is ever uncovered, it will merely confirm what is today a safe assumption.

An interesting aspect in Josephus's respectful comments on Jesus is his reference to the "tribe" of Christians that still existed in his day, some sixty years and more after the crucifixion. The Christian Church did not come into being structurally on the day James became Bishop of Jerusalem, even on the day Peter became Bishop of Rome. For a long time, Christians, whether Jews or Gentiles, had to exist in tribe-like pockets, either because they were isolated geographically or because persecution forced them to operate in secret. Either way, they were distinctly different from their neighbors, giving them further attributes of a tribe; either way, the lack of communication with other groups sometimes led one group into what can be called quasi-Christianity. For example, there existed in Syria around A. D. 125 an ultra Judaic tribe of Jewish Christians called Ebionites, named, according to tradition, after Ebion, who led them out of Jerusalem when the city fell in A. D. 70. The Ebionites rejected the writings of Paul on the grounds that he was too liberal with Jewish aspects of the religion, such as dropping the requirement of circumcision. Early Christians were sometimes called Nazarenes, after Nazareth, where Jesus spent part of His boyhood; but in the fourth century a tribe called the Nazarenes appeared in Persia. They, too, stressed the Jewish aspect of their Christianity and are thought by some scholars to be descendants of the Ebionites. The Nazarenes kept the Hebrew Sabbath as well as the Christian Sabbath; they, too, rejected Paul, and there was some division among them regarding the virgin birth.

Doubtlessly many such tribes existed from time to time and from place to place, their type of Christianity influenced by what they had been before, how well they were trained, and the circumstances that followed. There is recent evidence of this. Before the rise of Islam, Christian missionaries crossed North Africa, establishing thriving Christian communities from Cairo to Tangiers despite severe opposition. In fact, before the conversion of Constantine, there were more Christian martyrs at Carthage than in Rome. The westward spread of Islam put an end to Christianity in Mediterranean Africa for more than a thousand years. However, when, around 1870, French missionaries entered Algeria, they found in the mountains a tribe of Berbers who practiced a form of Christianity. Unlike the Moslems surrounding them, who regarded Jesus as a prophet only, these Berbers held Him to be the Messiah, they honored Mary, they had a form of communion service, and their properties were in common ownership—an early Christian custom. But they had adopted some Moslem traditions: facing eastward while praying five times a day, not drinking alcoholic beverages, and they practiced polygamy.

There has been an even more recent development that is pertinent. In March, 1970, two French scientists, Mr. and Mrs. Jean Bourgeois, came upon some writing on a rock outcropping near the town of Laghman in eastern Afghanistan, in a valley that was once the area's main east-west route. They took pictures of the writing and made casts of it and sent them to Professor Andre Dupont-Sommer, at the University of Paris, a man who had already gained fame for his translations of the Dead Sea Scrolls. Dupont-Sommer identified the writing as Aramaic, a Semite language which Jesus spoke, and the message made the writing something of a roadsign for a nearby Buddhist monastery. And because of the message, Dupont-Sommer was able to date the inscription to 250 B. C.

This is the background: At that time, the emperor of India was named Asoka, sometimes called Pryadarsi, and because of his wealth and his vast armies he was able to expand his kingdom westward into the Middle East. He was then a Brahman. However, after realizing that his wars of expansion were causing great sufferings and death, he converted to Buddhism and adopted a policy of nonviolence. Now in peaceful expansion, he sent Buddhist missionaries westward, and they are known to have reached as far as Greece and Egypt. As they traveled, they established monasteries.

The inscription begins: "This Way To Tadmor." Tadmor was an oasis in Syria and was better known as Palmyra. The inscription: "In the year 10 the King Pryadarsi expelled vanity from among the prosperous, the friends of that which is frivolous and of the fishing of fish-creatures. At a distance of 200 'bows,' this way to the place called Tadmor."

Professor Dupont-Sommer has expressed the opinion that there was a Buddhist monastery at Tadmor in those days and that the Aramaic sign on the road was like a billboard advertisement addressed to Semite caravans which passed this way. Buddhist monasticism developed in the Sixth Century B. C. in the Orient, and Dupont-Sommer now believes that the monastic life was

105

probably introduced into the Middle East either by Buddhist missionaries or by Semitic caravaners who had stopped for rest at Buddhist monasteries like the one at Tadmor.

He has said: "Shortly afterward, in the Second Century B. C., one sees appearing within the Jewish world robust institutions of the monastic type, based like the Buddhist monastic communities on celibacy, poverty, obedience. I refer to the Essenes of Palestine and the Therapeutae of Alexandria. For a long time one has been wondering about the origin of these Jewish mystic brotherhoods which had no precedent, no true model, in either the tradition of ancient Judaism or elsewhere in the Mediterranean world."

The Edgar Cayce Readings, on the other hand, suggest that the monastic traffic might have moved in the opposite direction, originating on Mount Carmel, spreading out as, like the early Christians, new groups were formed, perhaps changing the format a little, either disappearing or thriving, and with new groups unfolding outward from the old. During a Reading conducted by Hugh Lynn Cayce on May 5, 1941, this exchange took place:

Hugh Lynn: "Was the main purpose of the Essenes to raise up people who would be fit channels for the birth of the Messiah who later would be sent out into the world to represent the Brotherhood?"

Edgar: "The individual preparation was the first purpose. The being sent out into the world was secondary. Only a very few held to the idea of the realization in organization, other than that which would come with the Messiah's pronouncements."

Hugh Lynn: "Were the Essenes called at various times and places Nazarites, School of the Prophets, Hasidees, Therapeutae, Nazarenes, and were they a branch of the Great White Brotherhood, starting in Egypt and taking as members Gentiles and Jews alike?"

Edgar: "In general, yes. Specifically, not altogether. They were known at times as some of these—or the Nazarites were a branch of a THOUGHT of same, see? Just as in the present one would say that any denomination by name is a branch of the Christian-Protestant faith, see? So were those of the various groups, though their purpose was of the first foundations of the prophets as established—or as understood from the School of Prophets—by Elijah, and propagated and studied through the things begun by Samuel. The movement was NOT an Egyptian one, though ADOPTED by those in another period—or an earlier period—and made a part of the whole movement. They took Jews and Gentiles alike as members, yes."

Hugh Lynn: "Please describe the associate membership of the women in the Essene brotherhood, telling what privileges and restrictions they had, how they joined the Order, and what their life and work was."

Edgar: "This was the beginning of the period when women were considered as equals with the men in their activities, in their abilities to formulate, to live, to be, channels (for souls). They joined by dedication—usually by their parents. It was a free will thing all the way through, but they were restricted only in the matter of certain foods and certain associations in various periods —which referred to the sex as well as to the food or drink."

Hugh Lynn: "How did Mary and Joseph first come in contact with the Essenes and what was their preparation for the coming of Jesus?"

Edgar: "As indicated, by being dedicated by their parents."

Hugh Lynn: "Please describe the process of selection and training of those set aside as holy women, such as Mary, Editha and others, as a possible mother for the Christ. How were they chosen, were they mated, and what was their life and work while they waited in the Temple?"

Edgar: "They were first 'dedicated,' and then there was the choice of the individual through the (spiritual) growths, as to whether they would be merely channels for general services. For these (holy women) were chosen for special services at various times, as were the twelve chosen at the time (of Mary)—which may be used as an illustration. Remember, these (holy women) came down from the periods when the school had begun, you see.

107

"When there were the activities in which there were to be the cleansings through which bodies were to become channels for the new race, or the new preparation, these then were restricted—of course—as to certain associations (marriages), developments in associations, activities and the like. We are speaking here of the twelve women, you see, and all of the women from the beginning who were dedicated as channels for the new race, see?

"Hence the group we refer to here as the Essenes was the outgrowth of the periods of preparations from the teachings by Melchizedek, as propagated by Elijah and Elisha and Samuel. These were set aside for preserving themselves in direct line through which there might come the new or the Divine Origin, see?

"Their life and work during such periods of preparation were given to alms, good deeds, missionary activities, as would be termed today."

Hugh Lynn: "Please tell of the contacts of Thesea, Herod's third wife, with the Essenes, her meeting with one of the Essene wise men, and what were the names of the two wives preceding her?"

Edgar: "There was the knowledge of same (Essenes) through the giving of information by one of those in the household who had been so set aside for active service. Through the manner and conduct of life of that individual, and the associations and activities, the entity gained knowledge of that group's activities."

Hugh Lynn: "Please describe the Essene wedding, in temple, of Mary and Joseph, giving the form of ceremony and customs at that time."

Edgar: "This followed very closely the forms outlined in (the Book of) Ruth. It was not in any way a supplanting but a cherishing of the sincerity of purpose in the (Essenic) activities of individuals.

"When there was to be the association, or the wedding, of Joseph and Mary—Mary having been chosen as the channel by the activities indicated upon the stair, by the hovering of the angel, the enunciation to Anna and to Judy and to the rest of those in charge of the preparations at that time—then there was to be sought out the nearer of kin, though NOT in the blood relationships.

108

Thus the lot fell upon Joseph, though he was a much older man compared to the age ordinarily attributed to Mary in the period. Thus there followed the regular ritual in the temple. For, remember, the Jews were not refrained from following their rituals. Those of the other groups, as the Egyptians or the Parthians, were not refrained from following the customs to which they had been trained, where were not carried on in the Jewish temple but rather in the general meeting place of the Essenes as a body-organization."

During the Israeli-Arab Six-Day War in 1967, the Palestine Archaeological Museum in Old Jerusalem was a prime Israeli target. Israeli troops reached the building on the first day of the fighting, June 5, and found it well fortified by the Arabs. Within twenty-four hours, however, the Arabs were routed, and a sign was placed over the main door that this was now a museum of the State of Israel. Because of continuing danger, Israeli scholars were not able to enter the building until June 12, two days after the ceasefire. The main display room was a mess, with showcases broken and scroll fragments strewn about. At first, the main body of the scrolls, in the form of thousands of fragments, could not be found, and it was presumed that the Jordanians had earlier taken them away because of the threatening war. But then, during the cleaning up, a large display cabinet was moved away from the wall where it stood, and there was a safe. In it was everything the Jordanians had accumulated over the years except, perhaps significantly, the copper scrolls listing the hidden treasure. Still present at the museum were two French priest-scientists—Pierre Benoit and Roland de Vaux—who had supervised the Jordanian work from the start and who had earned positions of great honor in their fields. Their first impression was that the Israelis would move everything to their own facilities at the Hebrew University and take over the translating themselves, excluding them from their life's work. General Yadin promptly assured them that he wanted them to stay on and to continue their work there, in the new museum of the State of Israel. Then silence.

Even now, almost twenty-five years after the bulk of the Qumran documents was discovered, just about half of the material has been translated and published. This is not to suggest any efforts at secrecy, though some secrecy there has been. But there has also been a lack of money. There has been war. And there has been the job itself, of necessity a slow and tedious job. At times, Kando, the Bethlehem cobbler, would arrive with two or three fragments in a matchbox. Other times, he would arrive with fragments by the bushel. The Qumran caves have been generous. One cave—Cave Four—has produced all or parts of four hundred different manuscripts. But parts of the same manuscript have been found in three or four different caves, arriving at the museum months, even years, apart. Obviously the chore of piecing together all the fragments, some of them badly damaged, has demanded the utmost scientific detective work by the French priests and their staff.

It was, in fact, the detective work of Father de Vaux that led to the uncovering of the Qumran monastery, which for so long had been mistaken for an old Roman fort. During the excitement following the discovery of the first Scrolls, the priest went to Qumran to make his own inspection of the caves. What he saw led him to dismiss the prevalent theory that the caves had been repositories for discarded sacred books which had been written somewhere else, Jerusalem perhaps. The place simply was too remote, too difficult to reach, even for the most devout Jerusalem Jews to go to all that trouble. De Vaux also dismissed the possibility that the scrolls had been written in the caves. By summer day, the caves were unbearable hot ovens, and even the most dedicated scribe could not have worked in them for more than a few minutes at a time. De Vaux looked down at what he knew was supposed to be a Roman fort, and he wondered.

The excavation took three years, and what was finally uncovered had clearly been a monastery, a house of studies. The central building was about one hundred and twenty-five feet square and was a complex of rooms, passageways and cisterns. There were seven inside cisterns in all, which may have had some mystical significance. A two-story tower, with three-foot walls, stood on the northeast face of the building and was probably a watchtower. An aqueduct brought water down from the hills to a walled reservoir. There were enclosed courts, one of which may have been a stable. The main bulding had an assembly hall, a library, a scriptorium, a refectory and—judging from the coins found—an accounting office. There was a kitchen, an indoor oven, and in the pantry were found over a thousand bowls and jars. There were latrines, a communal washroom and several storerooms. Outside the main building but within the walls was a pottery with a kiln. Sherds indicate that the jars made here were the same as those found containing scrolls in the caves. Near the east end of the main building is a crack, clear through, showing a twenty-inch drop of the outer portion, caused, most likely, by the earthquake which is known to have occurred here in 31 B. C. The absence of roofing substances suggests that the roof was made of reeds that grew along the sea. The absence of living quarters suggests that the occupants of the monastery lived in tents outside the walls. On the compound has been found a mysterious wall, dating back to 700 B. C., but because it does not appear to have any relation to the monastery Father de Vaux concluded that there was no association between the two structures.

Judging from the coins found in and around the building, occupancy probably began around 136 B. C. Because some of the scrolls found in the caves are older than that, they must have been brought in from some other similar settlement. There is a gap in the dated coins between 37 B. C. and 4 B. C., and this may have been the period when, because of the earthquake, the Essenes went somewhere else. Found nearby was a time-buried mound of rubble, which gives the impression that the damaged part of the building was cleaned out when the people returned. Identifiable coins then proceed to A. D. 68, the eve of the fall of Jerusalem. There is a gap then of about sixty years, the later coins being of the period of Bar-Kochba's unsuccessful revolt against the Romans, at which time refugees might have occupied the monastery. Among the early fragments found in the caves by Father de Vaux was part of a letter from Bar-Kochba to a military officer, complaining about the lack of support he was getting from the "Gallileans" for the revolt. The pacifists must surely have been Christians.

The Manual of Discipline demonstrates that daily life in the monastery was austere and strict, but both Josephus and Philo attest to the fact that the Essenes were a happy, industrious and optimistic people. They were also clean. The Manual and the archaeological evidence shows that they washed several times a day, not merely as ritual but in the course of turning from one task to another. They had special clothes for their two meals a day, one at eleven in the morning, the other after sunset. Novices were not allowed to eat with the regular members for three years, their cleansing period; they were not to have any contact with the food or drink for others, and they even had to defecate in a separate place. For food and drink, the Manual mentions only bread and must or wine, but it is known that the Essenes farmed and kept herds. Since they did not offer animals as sacrifices, as did other Jews, the animal bones found at Qumran probably mean that the Essenes ate meat, at least on occasion. Moreover, the Manual applies to life at the monastery. Essenes living elsewhere undoubtedly led the usual daily life of devout Jews of their time.

Both Josephus and Philo comment on the silence at Qumran, but this would be proper demeanor in any monastery, any house of serious study, even today. The members were not to argue or bear grudges or be critical of anyone to others. If a disagreement developed, the two involved were first to discuss it between themselves. If they reached no compromise, a third person was to listen to a second discussion and try to settle the matter. This failing, the two went before the council of twelve elders and three priests, where the decision was final. (In Matthew 18: 15-17, Jesus gives the same instructions for settling differences.) Punishments for infractions could be severe: for speaking brusquely "so as to undermine the composure of a fellow" the offender's food ration was cut for a year; for falling asleep or spitting in a public session it was cut for a month. Then why was everybody so happy? Probably because they were convinced that of their own free will they were involved in something important, something important to them as individuals, to their sect, their religion and to their country, which were indivisible for them, and to mankind.

The Edgar Cayce Readings present a much broader panorama of Essenic life and the Essenic influences on Jesus, all disclosed while giving information on past incarnations of people who had requested the reading. For a while, Hugh Lynn Cayce, who witnessed thousands of Readings, was perturbed by the reports because so many of the people requesting them turned out to be either personages of high stature in their past or were intimately involved in important moments in history. Few seemed to be farmers or shopclerks or servants. There were exceptions to this generality, of course, many of them, but the Readings did seem to indicate that a lot of people who were just ordinary people today were celebrities two thousand years ago or at least friends of celebrities. Edgar Cayce couldn't argue the point; he could not claim accountability for the information that came from him during trance. But he did suggest some possible explanations.

The Essenes, it would appear, were well aware of their role in the Messianic destiny, and they had been, regardless of what they were called, for a long time. They were aware, too, at least some of them were, of the Caycean definition of souls and the soul's choice of the body it enters for another sojourn. As had been indicated in the Readings, a soul, having benefited spiritually, so to speak, during a particular sojourn, would often choose to return to human form in the same circumstances, even into the same family, with the hope of benefiting even more. Thus it was not uncommon for the Readings to show that many people who consulted Edgar Cayce had known each other in previous incarnations and had even been related in previous incarnations, though in different ways, in terms of husband and wife and parent and child. Because of its "twinness," a soul could enter either a male or female, though usually the soul remained of the gender of its first incarnation on earth. If, in one incarnation, the body entered became that of a celebrity, while, in another, the body became a John Doe, this did not matter greatly to the soul, which had principally been

113

seeking a vessel toward perfection, and this could be achieved at any social level. The world changed; the ways of life changed; perhaps souls were now seeking perfection along the simpler paths.

Another area of concern for both Hugh Lynn and Edgar Cayce was the inescapable fact that for many who came or wrote for Readings the interest in the phenomenon—in the "psychic" or the "occult," if you will— was more of a phase, a fad, even a fake. On a number of occasions, Edgar Cayce, during trance, scolded someone whose intentions became revealed as unworthy of his efforts. These people were unavoidable because they could not be recognized ahead of time, and the worst thing about them was that, out of their own dissatisfaction, they could cast discredit upon the work and thus discourage someone who was sincere. And most people were sincere. Those with health problems usually turned to Cayce as a last resort, after their doctors could do no more or do nothing at all. And those who sought Life Readings often were people who were trying to resolve a certain inner disquiet which might have been stirred by the soul's efforts to express itself in the subconscious, in a dream, or in that eerie sensation, called déjà vu, when you find yourself wondering if what had just happened had happened before or had been a dream. For these people, the Readings could be very helpful. They did not have to believe the information that was given; they could put aside any of the information that conflicted with what they already believed; but what they did accept usually granted them a certain peace, a certain knowledge, a certain guidance.

Certain information, in fact, conflicted with widespread beliefs and was, of itself, unorthodox, perhaps heretical for some, and the Cayces were also sensitive on these points, anxious not to offend or scandalize anyone. For example, numerous Readings state, in one way or another, that after Jesus was about ten years old and away at His studies with the Essenes, Mary and Joseph entered a normal marriage relationship and had three children of their own, two boys and a girl. The Roman Catholic Church, for which Edgar Cayce had such great respect and admiration, has traditionally held that Mary remained a virgin throughout her life. Theologians will probably debate this from now to the Omega. Yet there are other areas regarding Mary in which the Catholic position and the Readings' information are somewhat in tune. Catholic theologians have referred to Mary as the Second Eve; the Readings suggest that as the twin-soul of the entity who was both Adam and Jesus, she would be. The Catholic Church regards Mary as the co-Redemptress of mankind; the Readings would agree, on the same grounds. The Church considers Mary to be the mediatrix of all graces; the Readings would concur, and again on the same grounds. If, then, there is indeed anything in the Readings which might be offensive to anyone, whatever his beliefs, the fact the Edgar Cayce was unconscious while giving them might minimize the effects. If so, what then evolves is a staggering drama of a holy conspiracy the likes of which the world may never see again.

On February 24, 1932, Edgar Cayce had the occasion to add a letter to the transcript of a Life Reading he was sending to an inquirer who had requested it, and he said: "I am hoping that the information proves to be just that needed for you at this time. It is quite often hard for us to judge what is answered and what isn't answered satisfactorily. It may appear so to us, when it doesn't answer to the individual seeking at all." This concern was typical of the man throughout his life. He saw no reason for the Readings, no purpose for his faculty, unless it was to serve for the good of others seeking guidance, especially spiritual guidance. He often worried when there was no follow-up on a Life Reading or when a follow-up ceased. As far as he was concerned, he was giving people information, but he knew many of them were taking it as advice, and so it was important to him to know that people who had made inquiries of him and through him were well. For this reason he maintained a large correspondence, becoming friends with people who had come to him as strangers.

Once during trance Cayce was asked if the Readings should ever be made public, if they should be published. He said yes, but he said they should be edited. Cayce's utterances during trance were taken down in shorthand verbatim by Gladys Davis. He made no effort to dictate, in terms of organized sentences or thoughts, with the result that, though it must have been fascinating to listen to him, it is today often difficult to read him. Sometimes one sentence goes on endlessly, with two or three different thoughts included, requiring a jungle of punctuation which makes the Readings something that cannot be skimmed. Though Cayce was sometimes vague and sometimes changed minor details, he was impressively consistent, particularly in view of the fact that Readings on the same historic event or personage were often done as much as fifteen or twenty years apart. How much good the Readings achieved for the individuals who requested them will obviously never be established. The value of the Readings today is in the information they offer the student of Cayce or of any of the subjects which came up during them. And the value is great.

Typed and photocopied transcripts of the Readings fill scores of looseleaf notebooks which line the walls of the library in the A.R.E. headquarters at Virginia Beach. Each Reading has a code number, for the sake of the privacy of the individual involved, and the Readings are filed chronologically in terms of the date when they were done. If an individual had follow-up Readings, all of them nevertheless are filed under one code number on the date of the first Reading. However, references to a specific historic event or personage are scattered throughout the Readings, depending on the previous sojurns of the entity under consideration. It is in the course of weaving these scattered references into a historically chronological pattern that one becomes most aware of the consistency of the Readings.

For example, on May 18, 1924, very early in his experiences with Life Readings, Cayce informed a woman of fifty-five: "Before that we find the entity in the Holy Land when there were those admonitions being given just before the entering by the lawgiver, Moses. The entity was then among the children of Elijah the Priest, in the name then Miriam, and the entity became one to whom those in active service in the temple harkened." Apparently two sojourns are indicated, one at the time of

116

Moses, in the thirteenth century B. C.; the other at the time of Elijah, in the eighth century B. C. This was Cayce's first reference to Elijah and the temple on Mount Carmel, and it is interpreted that Miriam was not an actual child of Elijah but among the children placed in the care of Elijah's prophets—the first Essenes.

Forty years later, Cayce made another reference to an entity of Elijah's time. This was on April 3, 1944, to a woman of sixty, and: "Before that the entity was in the Holy Land among those of the household of the prophet, during the period of Ahab's and Jezebel's rule in the land. The entity then was the daughter of that prophet, in the name of Adah. The entity knew trials; the entity knew the wrath of those surrounding the entity and those periods of turmoils and wickedness among those in high places. Yet the entity kept the faith through the period. The entity was acquainted with the activities of Jehu and the entity's sister. The entity kept the faith and saw the fulfilling of the prophet's words about Ahab, Jezebel and those people of that day. Hence the prophecies as well as the promises throughout the Book have meant and do mean much to the entity."

There was some discussion after the Reading on whether Adah was the daughter of Elijah, and Cayce thought not. He felt she was the daughter of Obadiah, the priest who was the major domo of King Ahab. As such, she most likely knew Elijah and was influenced by him. The woman's love of the Bible was indicative in Caycean terms. A person's interests, his talents, even his preferences in personal relationships can be carry-overs from a previous sojourn which was happy and spiritually beneficial. We are not, after all, accidents. We are part of a plan, and a part of us knows that.

SEVEN

There must have been a great deal of excitement on Mount Carmel as those in charge realized that the time had come to choose from among the girls in the school the twelve who were to be presented to the angel. The excitement must have been even greater on the bright morning Mary was chosen. It is not known whether, that morning, Joseph was also living there on the mountain. His age at the time of the marriage—thirty-six—suggests that he may have been for some time a member of the branch of Essenes who did not marry. Ordinarily he would have been married before twenty. Some exegetes think that the brothers and sister of Jesus were Joseph's children by a former marriage and that, therefore, Mary did remain a virgin all her life. However, the lengths to which the authors of the Bible go to establish Joseph's lineage all the way back to Adam would indicate that as much care was taken in choosing him for his role in the training of Jesus as was taken with Mary. It is also not known whether, at the time of the betrothal, Joseph, realizing that his monastic days were over, left Mount Carmel and went to Nazareth to start his carpentry shop and prepare a home for Mary or whether he had left earlier and was summoned back after the angel had made the choice. The Bible shows Joseph as being surprised to learn that the betrothed Mary was pregnant, and he at first refused to marry her. The Edgar Cayce Readings explain that Joseph was concerned mainly about what the neighbors might say. It figures that, as an Essene, Joseph would have known he was not to be the actual father of the Christus; and, as a devout Jew, living in a small town, it would have been understandable for him to get upset when he discovered that the Incarnation had preceded a marriage. It would have been only as an Essene that Joseph could have accepted the message from his soul-mind during a dream that events were proceeding according to the Divine Plan and that he should not resist his role: The Readings establish that the Essenes accepted dreams as a means for this kind of communication.

Cayce once did a Life Reading for a girl of seventeen who had a similar experience with a dream. This was on September 4, 1934 (649-1), and Cayce, pursuing the girl's former sojourns, said:

"Before that we find the entity was in that land known as the Holy Land during the period when there had been those people who had looked and longed for, been expectant of, the coming of the promise to a people who sought relief from the material bondage as well as from the spiritual activities of those that gormandized themselves and their own interests in the sale of privilege in the activities of those things that were of the letter of the law without the spirit thereof. The entity then was in the household—and of the sisters—that were in the temple with that one chosen as the channel through which the Spirit would manifest in the Holy One; hence a daughter of Elois or the priestess that pleased the Holy One in the Temple with Simeon.

"Then the entity, in the latter portion of the experience in that land, poined in that band who made for what would be termed in the present a prayer band or ladies' aid or circle that made the preparations for those that had separated themselves to become the followers of those peoples. And the entity then was with Simon Peter's mother, wife, the children of Zebedee and their families, as well as Thomas and Luke—for Luke and Thomas were brothers.

"In that experience the entity, in the name of Andra, gained throughout. And the entity aided in preparing much of that which came later, in the form of visualizing the paintings on the walls, the drawings that (then) might be carried hither and that became as banners that might be shown. Also (in preparing) the wrappings for the last of the anointing of the body of the Holy One— rather the wrappings than the spices, for Magdalene and Mary and Josie and the mother of the Lord prepared

119

these. The napkins that were about His head and those seals that were later made as raised figures did the entity prepare."

A year later, on August 8, 1935, Cayce did a follow-up for this girl, and she had some questions for him:

"Please explain my relation with Mary, the mother of Jesus."

"The activities then were as one of those who grew up with those affiliated in that order which bound together that particular group of individuals that were all associated at the time. To elucidate: In the preparation for the coming of the Son of man, there were those during those periods who joined in their efforts to consecrate their lives, their bodies, for a service, for a channel through which activities might be had for the perfecting, as it were, of the material channel through which such an expression of the Creative Forces might come into the earth, see? There were, then, twelve maidens in the temple —or of the *order* of the temple, who were dedicated for such preparation. The entity, then, was one of the twelve, so associated with Mary in the preparations."

"Was Elois, as mentioned in my Life Reading, and Anna, mentioned in the Bible, one and the same?"

"No. Anna was the 'older' or what would be termed the supervisor or what would be termed by some as the lady superior of the group at the time."

"Is that Elois on the earth plane now?"

"We will have to look and see. . . . We don't find her on the earth today."

"Please give the reason for my dream about the children on the double staircase."

"This might be interpreted by some in one way, others in another! In this particular experience, if this is experienced again it will for farther. For it was as the children —as self—on the staircase that led to the ordination— or coronation—room, in the dedicating of those twelve at the time that Mary was *indicated*—by the walking up the steps, with the other children on the other—as the one being chosen or led by the Spirit. This rather, then, an *experience*—not a dream! Pray that it may be thine experience again. Let the deeper self, the real self, enter into the deep meditation that the 'I am' consciousness may make more and more aware of how the purposefulness of the experience may be applicable in the activities of the entity in the present. This is most to be desired."

"What were the figures on the seals on the Head of the Master that I prepared?"

"The seals of the Holy One, as the seals of the son of David: the pear with the bell, with the pomegranates on either side."

"In which incarnation and how was I associated with my mother?"

"The closest association was at the time of the Master—then the daughter of the mother."

"With my father?"

"At the same period, though not the father—then was the father the priest."

In 1941, another young woman (2425) received information which placed her, too, on the mountain on the morning of the selection. Married, the twenty-one-year-old girl had lately found herself yearning to have a baby. In trance, Cayce told her:

"Before that—which has again come as an urge in the present experience of the entity—we find that the entity was in that land now called by some the Promised Land, during those days when there was the looking forward to the channels through which there was expected to be the coming of the Messiah. The entity was among those of that group chosen as ones to present themselves as a channel worthy of acceptance to be such. Hence in its youth, as well as through those periods of girlhood, motherhood, the entity knew many of those who were so active—as was the entity—in those periods for a DEFINITE religious experience, as would be called today.

"The entity then was of that sect or group known as the Essenes and of those who were of the house of David, but of the kinship little to Joseph or Mary—and yet of those same groups. The entity was among those who saw that vision on the stairs, when the first choice of the maidens was made. The entity knew then of the voice of the unseen forces as were aroused within the group that made for the speaking with the unusual tongues—not unknown yet unusual tongues—the ability to make known their wishes to many in many tongues.

121

"Throughout that experience the entity gained, though—as many that were of definite groups that set metes and bounds for their activities in relation to groups or masses or even individuals—there were periods when the entity doubted. But with the advancing of the activities which brought about the fulfilling to the entity of the various experiences, that answered to all phases of not only the material but the spiritual and mental phenomena, the entity was a believer and among those who in the last day stood at the Cross. The name then was Sophie.

"As to the activities in the present, let those things which have—and do—come be controlled by what thy ancestors have given as religious experiences, and not merely phenomena. For phenomena—or phenomenon—is but an awakening to that in which there ARE to be choices of activity upon the part of the self and is as an assurance and not to be boasted of, nor to be other than that of the ANSWERING to that within. For thy body —as ye experienced then—is indeed the temple of the living God, and there He hath promised to meet thee. There His awareness—even as then—may be seen, may be heard, may be felt, may be tasted—yea, experienced in all manners. But the reality is to self, not to others. For of thyself ye may do nothing; but as His spirit, His truth, may work in and through thee, ye may indeed be a channel, a blessing, a way for others to become aware of THEIR relationship also to that divine experience."

The woman asked: "Is there any reason I should not conceive a child now? What can I do to help me in this?"

Cayce said: "No. This, as we find, needs only that care, that attention, which was given as a part of thy development through that Palestine period; that is: a body strong in the activity of accomplishment in physical strength, a mind attuned to Creative Forces, and an attitude of: 'Father-God! Use me as a channel of blessings to others; teaching me, in body, in mind, the manner or way to project such as would be given me, that they may become greater blessings in glorifying thee.' "

There was no follow-up, so it is not known whether the woman ever had children. But what is significant about the Reading was the fact that, having once spent

122

several years in intensive preparation for the possibility of being the chosen maiden, this woman's soul-mind still carried the deep desire to be the channel. Of course, the woman's desire to have a child could be described as her natural "mother" instinct; even so, the nature of instincts is still a mystery to scientists.

A remarkable woman who played a major role in the Essene life and in the training of Jesus came to light during Readings that began in November, 1937, and continued intermittently for almost a year. She was then fifty-seven years old. Her name, of course, is secret; she was Reading 1472. She appears to have been a professional woman; she refers to her job, and she was interested in writing, either as a hobby or professionally. Perhaps it was because of her prominence among the Essenes that her name comes up in other Readings. Indications are that she knew others who were going to Cayce for Readings—knew them in 1937 and during the Essene era—but her name also appears in the Readings of others whom she did not know in recent times. From her role with the Essenes, it would appear that she had something to do with the Dead Sea Scrolls. Without question, she was a woman of influence and leadership. During the first Reading, on November 6, Cayce gave her this information:

"Before that we find the entity was in the Palestine land during those days when the Master walked in the earth and when there were the people (going) about those activities of not only the birth but His sojourns before and after the return from Egypt—those whom Judy blessed, that labored in the preserving of the records of His activities as the Child, the activities of the Wise Men, the Essenes and the groups to which Judy had been the prophetess, the healer, the writer, the recorder, for all of these groups. And though questioned or scoffed by the Roman rulers and the tax gathered—and especially those that made for the levying or the providing for those activities of taxation, the entity gained throughout.

"Though the heart and body was often weary from the toils of the day and the very imprudence—yea, the very selfishness of others for the aggrandizing of their bodies rather than their souls or minds seeking development—

123

the entity grew in grace, in knowledge, in understanding. And in the present those abilities arise from its desire, from its hopes, to put into the word of the *day* the experiences of the day in all phases of human experiences; *lessons*—yea, symbols; yea, tenets—that will drive, as it were, *home* in those periods when the soul takes thought and counsel with itself, as to whence the experiences of the day are leading, as to whether they are leading to those activities that are the fruits of the spirit of truth and life or to those that make for selfishness and the aggrandizement of material appetites, without thought of those things that are creative and only make the pure growths within the experience of others.

"Hence whether it be in jest, in stories, in song or poem or whether in skits that may show the home life, the lover; yea, the weary traveler; yea, the high-minded, and they that think better of themselves than they ought to think, *these* abilities are there. Use them. For He, even as then, will bless thee with His presence in same. And what greater assurance can there be in the experience of any soul than to know that He—yea, the Son of Mary; yea, the Son of the Father, the Maker of heaven and earth, the Giver of all good gifts—will be thy right hand; yea, thy heart, thy mind, thy heart itself, if ye will hold fast to Him."

The woman asked: "Where, when and what was my relationship to the entity now known as (1470) in any past incarnation, and what does he mean to my present life pattern?"

Cayce said: "In the Palestine period the self was Judy; the entity (1470) was as the Roman that made light much but later came to seek. And thus in authority in self doth he find that those activities in the present will become much in the same way and manner. For not as one dependent upon the other but one as bolstering, as it were, the purposes that may be held aright."

The woman: "Where, when and what was my past relationship to the entity now known as (1151), and what is the purpose of my present association with him?"

"In the same land. Here we find quite a variation in the activity. For as the entity that walked in the way to Emmaus *found* that those records of those activities be-

124

came part and parcel of the experience, so is that bond of sympathy found in the associations that awakens the urge for a *helpfulness without question* as one to another." (The "entity" here is the Risen Jesus, who, walking one night to Emmaus, seven miles east of Jerusalem, explained to two disciples who did not recognize Him how all the prophecies regarding the Messiah had now been fulfilled.)

On November 18, No. 1472 returned to the Cayce home for more information about her Essenic incarnation, and Cayce surprised those present by disclosing, in trance, that the information then available to him was coming from records which Judy herself had written at that time. And he said:

"Some four and twenty years before the advent of that entity, that soul-entrance into the material plane called Jesus, we find Phinehas and Elkatma making those activities among those of the depleted group of the prophets in Mount Carmel, (activities) begun by Samuel, Elisha, Elijah, Saul and those during those early experiences. Because of the divisions that had arisen among the people into sects, as the Pharisee, the Sadducee and their divisions, there had arisen the Essenes that had cherished not merely the conditions that had come as word of mouth but had kept the records of the periods when individuals had been visited with the supernatural or out of the ordinary experiences, whether in dreams, visions, voice or what-not, that had been and were felt by these students of the customs, of the law, of the activities throughout, the experiences of this peculiar people—the promises and the many ways these had been interpreted by those to whom the preservation of same had been committed.

"Hence we find Phinehas and the companion, both having received the experience similar to that received by Hannah and Elkanah, had drawn aside from many of the other groups. And then, as in answer to that promise, the child—Judy—was born. That the entity was a daughter, rather than being male, brought some disturbance, some confusion, in the minds of many. Yet the life, the experience of the parents, had been such that still—fulfilling their promise—they brought the life of

125

their child, Judy, and dedicated it to the study and the application of self, to the study of those things that had been handed down as part of the EXPERIENCES of those who had received visitations from the unseen, the unknown, or that worshiped as the Divine Spirit moving into the activities of men.

"Hence we find the entity Judy was brought up in that environment not of disputations, not of argumentations, but rather as that of rote and writ—as was considered necessary for the development, the influences, the activities of the life, to induce or to bring about those experiences. That much had been to that period as tradition, rather than as record, appeared—from the activity of the entity Judy—to have made a great impression. So there was the setting about to seek means and manners for the preservation and for the making of records of that which had been handed down as word of mouth, as tradition. Such channels and ways were sought out. And eventually the manner was chosen in which records were being kept in Egypt, rather than in Persia, from which much of the tradition arose, of course, because of the very indwelling of the peoples in that land.

"Hence not only the manners of the recording but also the traditions of Egypt, the traditions from India, the conditions and traditions from many of the Persian lands and from many of the borders about same, became a part of the studies and the seeking of the entity Judy early in the attempts to make, keep and preserve such records. The manners of communication being adverse, owing to the political situations that gradually arose due to the Roman influence in the land, made more and more a recluse of the entity in its early periods, until there were those visitations by what ye call the Wise Men of the East—one from Persia, one from India, one from the Egyptian land. They reasoned with the Brethren, but more was sought from the studies of the entity Judy at that experience.

"Then there was the report by the Wise Men to the king. Has it been thought of or have you heard it reasoned as to why the Wise Men went to Herod, who was only second or third in authority, rather than to the Romans who were ALL authority in the land? Because of Judy, knowing that this would arouse in the heart and mind of this debased ruler—who only sought for the aggrandizement of self—such reactions as to bring to him, this despot, turmoils with those then in authority. Why? There was not the proclamation by the Wise Men, neither by Judy nor the Essenes, that this new kind (king?) was to replace Rome! It (He?) was to replace the Jewish authority in the land!

"Thus we find, as it would be termed in the present, attention was called or pointed to the activity of the Essenes, such that, a little later—during those periods of the sojourn of the Child in Egypt because of same, Herod issued the edict for the destruction. This brought to those that were close to the entity those periods that were best described by the entity itself, in the cry of Rachel for her children that were being born into a period of opportunity, but the destructive forces, by the very edict of this tyrant, made them as naught.

"Hence during those periods of the ministry of John and then of Jesus, more and more questioning was brought upon the recorder—or Judy—by the Roman authorities or the Roman spies or those who were the directors of those who collected and who registered taxes of those people for the Roman collection. Consequently, we find the entity came in contact with the Medes, the Persians, the Indian influence or authority because of the commercial association as well as the influence that had been upon the world by those activities of Saneid and those that were known during the periods of Brahma and Buddha. These brought to the experience of the entity the weighing of the counsels from the traditions of the Egyptians and of her own kind, and then that new understanding.

"Hence we find the entity in those periods soon after the Crucifixion not only giving comfort but a better interpretation to the Twelve, to the Holy Women, an understanding as to how Woman was redeemed from a place of obscurity to her place in the activities of the affairs of the race, of the world, of the empire—yea, of the home itself. Those all became a part of the entity's experiences during that portion.

"Hence we find many have been, many are, the contacts the entity has made and must make in this present experience. For, as then, the evolution of man's experiences is for the individual purpose of becoming more and more acquainted with those activities in the relationships with the fellow man, as an exemplification, as a manifestation, of Divine Love, as was shown by the Son of Man, Jesus: that *each* and every soul *must become, must be*, the *savior* of some soul to even *comprehend* the purpose of the entrance of the Son INTO the earth—that man might have the closer walk with, yea, the open door to, the very heart of the living God!

"The entity's activities during the persecutions aroused much in the minds of those that made war again and again upon the followers of the Nazarene, of Jesus, of the Apostles here and there. And the entity, as would be termed, was hounded, yea, was persecuted the more and more; yet remaining until what ye would call the sixty-seventh year *after* the Crucifixion or until Time itself began to be counted from same. For the records as were borne by the entity, it will be found, were *begun* by the activities of the entity during what ye would term a period of sixty years *after* the Crucifixion. And then they were reckoned first by the peoples of Carmel, next by the brethren in Antioch, then a portion of Jerusalem, then to Smyrna, Philadelphia, and those places where these (Essenic Christians) were becoming more active. The entity—though receiving many rebuffs; yea, even stripes in the body—died a natural death in that experience, at the age of ninety-one.

"As to the associations, the lessons that are to be gained in the applications of self from that experience: Many are the urges that arise, as indicated; many are the impulses oft to feel that the very knowledge puts self in a position to condemn. But condemn not, even as He did not condemn.

"Again there are the inclinations that arise for abilities to present, to correlate, subjects that are truths hidden in tradition, hidden in prejudice of race, hidden in tradition of the patriotic influences that are accredited by the very spirit of a nation of people or a custom or a condition that has set itself in order as organizations. But gathering these, do not condemn. For know there is only ONE SPIRIT—that is the Spirit of Truth that has grown within same. For if there is the spirit of strife or the spirit of any activities that bring contention or turmoils, it takes hold upon these very fires that ye have so *well* put away, but that keep giving, giving, urges that are spoken of, even as He that ye *know*—that the prince of this world is as a raging lion, going about seeking whom He may destroy.

"What is this spirit, then, of unrest but that very cry, as He gave in that triumphal entry, 'If ye did not cry, "Hosanna, glory to the Lord, the King of kings," the very stones would cry out!' That these overreach themselves, ye have seen in the great white light of thine understanding, of the many *varied* feelings, yea, the varied approaches ye have seen. Does it become any wonder to thee, knowing, feeling, that ye have known these experiences, that ye have heard many a voice raised here and there, cry: 'Lo, here am I. Lo, here is my way. Lo: Listen.'

"But rather as those promises, yea, as thy very self hath *pronounced*: 'It is the still small voice within that finds communion with that Spirit that beareth witness that thy interpretation be true,' that all the prophets pronounced Him as that star spoken of, as that voice raised in the wilderness, as the star of Jacob, yea, of the household of David, yea, as of Judah that lion that will bring that as He declared unto the world—'My peace I leave with thee.'

"That ye declared; that hold to! For there *is* no other way than that each soul be awakened to that ye did proclaim to the earth: 'Behold He cometh with power and might and ye shall know him as He *is*: for He convicts thee of thy purpose among thy fellow men!' "

Cayce was ready for questions, and the woman wanted to know: "How close was my association with Jesus in my Palestine sojourn?"

"A portion of the experience the entity was the teacher," Cayce said. "How close? So close that the very heart and purposes were proclaimed of those things that were traditions! For the entity sent Him to Persia, to Egypt, yea, to India, that there might be completed the more perfect knowledge of the material ways in the activities of Him that became the Way, the Truth!"

She asked: "How can I extend the scope of my writing opportunity to use this ability in more important channels and wider service than at present?"

Cayce said: "As may be gathered from that as given, by putting into first thine own experience, thine own activity, those teachings of Him not as tenets but as *living* experiences. So manifesting same in the lives and minds of those whom the self may meet day by day, learning that lesson as He so well manifested, that it was not in the separation as John, not in the running away as Elijah, not as in sitting in high places as Isaiah, not as in that form of Jeremiah—mourning, not in that lording of Moses .but *all things unto all men,* reaching them in their own plan of experience and not with long-facedness.

"For as He—He wined, He dined with the rich; He consorted with the poor, He entered the temple on state occasions; yea, He slept in the field with the shepherds; yea, He walked by the seashore with the throngs, He preached to those in the mount—*all things;* and yet ever ready to present the tenets, the truths, even in those forms of tales; yea, parables; yea, activities, that took hold upon the *lives of men and women* in *every* walk of human experience.

"So ye will find that the lessons ye gave then may be used today. Why? Because Truth is *Truth, ever*—in *whatever stage,* in whatever realm of evolution, in *whatever* realm ye find same. It is as He gave: the little leaven. Think not, even as He, to do some great deed that would make the welkin ring throughout the earth. Rather *know* it is the little line, the little precept, the little lesson given into the lives and experiences that brings the awareness into the hearts and souls of men and women, that consciousness of the *nearness* in the still small voice within. For as proclaimed of old, it is not in the thunder or lightning, it is not in the storm, it is not in the loudness, but the still small voice within.

"So as ye write, so as ye talk, so as ye love, let it be in meekness of spirit, in *purposefulness* of service, in an activity and an eye single to the *glory* of the Father through those that are His children. For 'Who is my mother, my brother, my sister? They that do the will of

130

the Father, the same is my mother, my brother, my sister.' What is the will? Love the Lord with all thy heart, thy mind, thy body; thy neighbor as thyself! *Sow* the seeds of kindness, helpfulness, longsuffering, gentleness, patience, brotherly love, and leave the *increase* to the Father, who *alone* can give same either in the spirit, the mind OR the body. Being patient, even as He.

"This is the manner in which ye may reach—O the whole earth—even as ye did, Judy, in thy counsel as given thee by thy father in the flesh, as ye learned, as ye gathered, from the counsel of the lessons from the patriarchs of old, by the lessons of tradition that ye first —even as he—set to be in order; yea, have heard as of old, as eye for an eye, a tooth for a tooth; ye have heard he that does the good, do the good to him; but 'I say he that would smite thee on the right cheek, *turn thou* the other also! He that would sue thee and take away thy cloak, give him thy coat also.' Did ye not set these as the very words given by Him who is the Lord of Lords and the King of Kings? For to Him who hath overcome—and He standeth at the door and knocks—and *ye,* as all His servants, His children, His sisters, His brethren may be co-laborers with Him in the harvest that is ripe."

The woman wanted to know: "What is the purpose of my present business position and when will I be freed from it?"

Cayce said: "That ye may reach the more. Each experience, as ye will learn the more and more, as ye see them, just as given, is that ye may serve the better. For how gave He? 'He that is greatest among you is servant of all.' When shall ye be free from same? When ye have attained, when ye have gained, that next step, that He may say, 'Move on now, that thy children, those ye have taught, may carry on. Ye are called to the greater service of making known again—by word of mouth or by the pen—the greater lessons of Truth.' We are through for the present."

At another Reading, the woman asked directly: "If, as you have said, I was a prophetess, healer, teacher and writer in my Palestine sojourn, why does so-called sacred history give not record of me or my works?"

131

Equally direct, Cayce said: "Ye were of the Essenes, not of the Jews not even the Samaritans!"

Case 1472 opens wide areas for conjecture. Readings of others support the probability that she was the first Essene woman to attain such stature, and one reason for this could have been that the Caycean definition of the twinness of a soul might have been realized by the Essenes of that time and would have eradicated any inequality between the sexes. Her setting into order the traditions of the prophets can mean that she was responsible in some way for the recopying of the ancient documents which are now part of the Old Testament. She may, for that matter, have been one of the persons, perhaps the person, who decided what the commentary should be, in the way that some of the Qumran literature are commentaries. And yet she was also associated somehow with the New Testament. Repeatedly in the Readings, Cayce reminds her of things she had said or written, and they are from the Gospels. Exegetes have long agreed that the books of Matthew, Mark and Luke were written before the Fall of Jerusalem (A. D. 70), as much as ten years before. The Essenes were at Qumran at that time and could well have made copies of these writings to circulate among the growing and widely scattered Christian communities. There had been some uncertainty about the date of the Gospel by John. It is known that he was rather young, maybe a teen-ager, when Jesus chose him to become one of the Twelve, and that he lived to an old age, dying around A. D. 100 in the Grecian seaport of Ephesus, in what is now Turkey. John's complex symbolism, especially in his prologue, led some scholars to deduce that John wrote his account of Jesus in his old age after spending many years in discussions with symbolistic Greek philosophers. The discovery of the Dead Sea Scrolls changed that opinion. John is so definitely Essenic, particularly in his references to "the light" and "the darkness," that the prevalent opinion now is that he wrote much earlier, that he was familiar with Essenic writings and thought, and that he may have been an Essene himself. John came to know Jesus through John the Baptist; the experts are now confident that the Baptist was an Essene. All these events occurred while, according to the Readings, Judy was a powerful figure in the Essene movement and as such she would have been part of them. The Readings say she also set into order the records pertaining to Jesus, which could mean the Gospels, even later writings, perhaps in seeing to it that the events were put into writing by the men who were best acquainted with them and then supervising the editing and the copying.

Some questions arise. Why, indeed, was Judy not mentioned anywhere in the New Testament. Cayce said: "Ye were an Essene." The Essenes, of course, are mysteriously absent from the New Testament. It should be kept in mind, however, that this question was asked by a woman of our day, a woman to whom the Readings make several pointed remarks about the value of humility. Since each life experience unites a soul with a human personality with which it may exist either in harmony or conflict, depending on the human, it may be that this soul, during the sojourn as Judy, was united with a human whose conscious awareness of her divine mission enabled her to accept positions of prominent leadership while shunning personal notoriety. Judy appears to be that sort of woman.

And she evidently remained so. Without revealing Judy's identity, Hugh Lynn Cayce has said of her: "In the present life, she was the author and producer of several successful Broadway plays and entertainments imported from Europe. At different times in her life, she did two national radio programs. In another period, she did a syndicated column published in about a hundred newspapers. At still another time, she was involved with a United States tourist attraction. Talent and ability-wise, there was every reason for this lady to have been 'somebody' in the past." Many such people came to Edgar Cayce—men and women who were mature, intelligent and successful, and whose main interest in their past incarnations was to acquire information which would contribute to their spiritual development in the present.

Another question. If the Essenes were the first Christians, why aren't their documents after the birth and after the death of Jesus more specifically Christian? An-

133

other question. Why haven't any New Testament documents, per se, been found among the Qumran literature? There are all kinds of answers and, at this point, they must all be guesswork. Half of the Qumran literature has yet to be identified publicly, and it could contain all sorts of surprises. There could be early New Testament documents waiting to be found anywhere in that vast and lonely area known as the Middle East, taken there and hidden there by the early Christians as they fled from the Roman conquerors. Maybe this is why none of it has been found yet at the Dead Sea, or ever will be. For that matter, a Christian document, written within living memory of Jesus, probably wouldn't bear much more resemblance to Christianity today than do the documents we have—the New Testament. The first Christianity was a way of life. Today's Christianity is a way of worship. And there is a big difference.

The difference is made clear in the Edgar Cayce Readings. There was a tremendous sense of involvement among those first Christians—or whatever they called themselves. The Flight to Egypt is a good example of this. The Bible and traditional literature give a lonely picture of this event. Warned of Herod's edict by an angel, Mary and Joseph and the Child sneak away in the middle of the night and somehow manage to travel hundreds of miles across the bleak desert to a strange and friendless country where they remain in hiding until they are told that they can safely return. Not so, according to the Readings.

The Readings clearly show that the Essenic Christians —the Messianics, as they might say—were far too concerned about the safety of the Christus to let the Holy Family make that long and dangerous journey without careful planning and complete protection. Though the family traveled secretively, they were constantly under the surveillance of friends who either lived along the way or had been posted along the way as safeguards, and they lived among friends during the stay in Egypt. Though this at first may sound unorthodox, it can begin to sound reasonable when one wonders whether the Almighty God would entrust the Christus to an impoverished, small-town carpenter and a naive teen-aged girl, no matter how pious they were. Moreover, the suddenness with which the ministry of Jesus later began and grew supports the probability that a group of some size was working with Him.

Evidence of the extent to which the group made Him the center of their efforts appears impressively in the Readings for Mrs. 1010. This woman was in her sixties when she began asking Edgar Cayce to obtain information about her previous incarnations. On April 13, 1938, he told her:

"Before that we find the earthly sojourn of the great influence which should, or may, become one—if given individually as a period—that would lay the foundation for giving a great deal of historic data. Not that it would be *materially* helpful, but it would add to the information for the satisfying of individuals seeking an understanding as to those mysterious surroundings.

"For the entity's sojourn was during the period when the Master was born in the earth, in Bethlehem of Judea, of the city of Nazareth; and (at the time) when there had been the proclamation made by Herod for the destruction of the young, when Joseph had been warned to flee into Egypt, (so) that the prophecy might be fulfilled, 'Lo, my son has been called from Egypt' or 'Lo, the Messiah has been called from Egypt,' as given in Jeremiah as well as Isaiah.

"The entity then chose to join with the Holy Family and acted in the capacity of the handmaid to the mother, the Child, and waited on Joseph during those sojourns, dwelling by the brooks or the portions where there were wells in the upper portion of the Egyptian land to which they fled. During those periods of the journey the entity ministered, and it was no mean distance for a very young child and a very young mother during such delicate conditions.

"And the very ministering of the entity throughout that sojourn, first to the mother and to the Child and later to the aging Joseph, has caused those abilities which the entity finds in the present experience to minister to the needs of those ill in body, in mind. And such applications are those that may be made by the hand—nursing and care—and the consideration of the body as subsisting

135

upon *natural*, or Nature's, activities in the material world.

"In that experience the entity was known as Sophie—or Josie. She was close friends with the Innkeeper, who made preparations for the birth, because of his Essenic associations with the family to which the entity then joined, as part of the activities of the Essenes and the holy ones to protect the child. Through the experience the entity gained. And with the return to Capernaum and when the other children of the mother came, the entity still ministered.

"And with the activities of the growing child Jesus, His teachings and His ministerings became all a portion of the entity's experience; and yet she was so disturbed by the activity of others who were close and the manner in which these members of the (Essene) family deserted the teachings because of economic pressures that developed.

"In the application of self in the present respecting same, study those portions that have been written, again and again, and there will gradually come into the consciousness an awareness of the entity in the present that in Him is indeed the light that lightens the world and that only in just living His way may we indeed be like Him. Only may the awareness come in being that type of individual, with that purpose, with that attitude which He manifested ever. Though He came to His own and His own received Him not, never—*never*—did He rail at them. Never did He manifest any other than just gentleness, kindness, brotherly love, patience, with those who were the most unkind.

"The entity's activities, then, were even in the preservation of the keeping of the family intact, with the death of Joseph. For this the entity saw; closed the eyes and laid him to rest.

"Hence, as the entity reads of those activities there will come more and more an awakening. Read especially the first chapter of John; the first and second and third (epistles) of John. For the second epistle of John (as a letter) was directed to this entity, Josie, by John the beloved. Read then the fourteenth, fifteenth, sixteenth and seventeenth of John. And reading it, not as rote, ye will find that even He is speaking, even as to thee!"

During another Reading on this entity, on June 21, 1942, Cayce said:

"In giving the biographical life of the entity Josie, much of those activities might be indicated that brought about those later relationships with Mary, the mother of Jesus. As has been outlined from here, there were those special groups of individuals who had made some preparations for the expected activities that were to come about during that particular period, especially those of the Essenes who had chosen the twelve maidens to indicate their fitness. This choice was to be made by those selections indicated by the Spirit; and Josie was the daughter of Shem and Mephibosheth, who were among those.

"This entity, Josie, was close to Mary when the selection was indicated by the shadow or the angel on the stair, at that period of the consecration in the temple. This was not the temple in Jerusalem but the temple where those who were consecrated worshiped—or a school, as it might be termed, for those who might be channels. This was a part of that group of Essenes who, headed by Judy, made those interpretations of those activities from the Egyptian experience—as the Temple Beautiful and the service in the Temple of Sacrifice. Hence it was in this consecrated place where this selection took place.

"Then, when there was the fulfilling of those periods when Mary was espoused to Joseph and was to give birth to the Savior—the Messiah, the Prince of Peace, the Way, the Truth, the Light—soon after this birth there was the issuing of the orders, first by Judy, that there should be someone selected to be with the parents during their period of sojourn in Egypt. This was owing to the conditions which arose from the visit of the Wise Men and their not returning to Herod to report, when the decrees were issued that there should be the destruction of the children of that age from six months to two years, especially in that region from Bethany to Nazareth.

"Thus this entity, Josie, was selected or chosen by those of the Brotherhood—sometimes called White Brotherhood in the present—as the handmaid or companion of Mary, Jesus and Joseph in their flight into Egypt. This began on an evening, and the journey—through portions of Palestine, from Nazareth to the

137

borders of Egypt—was made only during the night. Do not understand that there were only Joseph, Mary, Josie and the Child. For there were other groups that preceded and followed, that there might be the physical protection to that as had been considered by these groups of people as the fulfilling of the Promised One.

"In the journeys to Egypt, little of great significance might be indicated; but the care and attention to the Child and the Mother was greatly in the hands of this entity, Josie, through that journey. The period of sojourn in Egypt was in and about or close to what was then Alexandria. Josie and Mary were not idle during that period of sojourn, but those records—that had been a part of those activities preserved in portions of the libraries there—were a part of the work that had been designated for this entity. And the interest in same was reported to the Brotherhood in the Judean country. The sojourn there was a period of some four years—four years, six months, three days.

"When there were these beginnings of the journey back to the Promised Land, there were naturally—from some of the records that had been read by the entity Josie, as well as the parents—the desire to know whether there were those unusual powers indicated in this Child now, who was in every manner a normal, developed body, ready for those activities of children of that particular period. But do not interpret same in the light of childhood in thine own land in the present—more in the light of the oriental. For, remember, Egypt as well as parts of Galilee were the customs and activities of those to whom the care of this physical entity was entrusted through that early sojourn in the earth.

"The return was made to Capernaum—not Nazareth, not only for political reasons due to the death of Herod but the division that had been made with the kingdom after the death of Herod, and also that there might be the ministry or teaching that was to be a part of the Brotherhood, supervised in that period by Judy as one of the leaders of the Essenes in that particular period. Hence much of the early education, the early activities, were those prompted or directed by that leader in that particular experience but were administered by—or in

138

the closer associations by—Josie. Though from the view of the Brotherhood the activities of the entity were no longer necessitated, the entity Josie preferred to remain. And she did remain until those periods when there was the sending or the administering of the teachings to the young Master, first in Persia and later in India and then in Egypt again, where there were the completions.

"But the entity Josie, following the return, was active in all the educational activities as well as in the care of the body and the attending to those things pertaining to the household duties with every developing child. And Josie was among those who went with Mary and Joseph when they went to the city—or to Jerusalem—at the time of the age of twelve. It was thought by Joseph and Mary that it was in the care of Josie that He had stayed, when He was missed, in those periods when there was the returning to find Him in the temple.

"Josie was with Mary throughout those activities. And is it any wonder that when there were those preparations of the body for burial that Josie was the one who brought the spices, the ointments, that were to consecrate the preparations of this body for whom it had cared through those early periods of its experiences in the earth? Through that period Josie never married and was known among the Holy Women throughout the period, coming and persuading the Mother Mary, when there was the arrest, to come to Jerusalem.

"The entity passed on through those periods of riots following the beheading of James, the brother of John. Ready for questions."

The woman wanted to know: "What was the nature of the records studied by Josie in Egypt?"

Cayce said: "Those same records of which the men of the East said and gave, 'By those records we have seen His star.' These pertained, then, to what you would call today astrological forecasts, as well as those records which had been compiled and gathered by all of those of that period pertaining to the coming of the Messiah. These had been part of the records from those in Carmel, in the early experiences, as those given by Elijah, who was the forerunner, who was the cousin, who was the Baptist. All of these had been a part of the records, pertaining not only to the nature of work of the parents but as to their places of sojourn and the very characteristics that would indicate these individuals, the nature and the character that would be a part of the experiences to those coming in contact with the young Child, even as to how the garments worn by the Child would heal children. For the body, being perfect, radiated that which was health, life itself. Just as today, individuals may radiate, by their spiritual selves, health, life, that vibration which is destruction to *dis*-ease in any form in bodies. These were the characters and natures of things studied by Josie.

"For, is it not quoted oft, 'All of these things she kept and pondered them in her heart.' With what? With the records that Josie as well as herself had seen. These records were destroyed, of course, in a much later period."

The woman: "Can any more details be given as to the training of the Child?"

Cayce: "Only those that covered the period from six years to about sixteen, which were in keeping with the tenets of the Brotherhood as well as that training in the law—which was the Jewish or Mosaic law in that period. This was read, this was interpreted, in accordance with those activities defined and outlined for the parents and the companions of the developing body. Remember and keep in mind: He was normal; He developed normally. Those about Him saw those characteristics that may be anyone's who wholly puts the trust in God. And to every parent might it not be said: Daily dedicate thy life that thy offspring may be called of God into service, to the glory of God and to the honor of thy name!"

EIGHT

There is evidence in the Qumran literature to suggest that the Essenes believed in reincarnation to some extent. The Teacher of Righteousness was to return to lead them to victory in the war between the Sons of Light and the Sons of Darkness. Other evidence suggests that the Essenes believed in the immortality of souls which had descended from the purest ethereal substance to be imprisoned in the body. Both these concepts can be encompassed, to a degree, by what perhaps can be called the Caycean philosophy. However, various scholars have attributed them to Greek and Persian influences upon earlier Jewish religious thought. The Essenes themselves wrote that their tenets had been presented to them by the Teacher of Righteousness upon reorganizing them as a group after a period of defusion.

The Cayce Readings support the idea of defusion. They show that the Essenes were the culminant group of a centuries-old sect among which there had been numerous differences and divisions; and it seemed that each time the movement became too diluted, some strong personality would appear to strengthen it again by means of special information, special awareness. Then the sect would regain its sense of purpose and direction: the broken chain would become one again.

The broken chains are still being made one. Like this. Josephus mentions, almost in passing, that on the plain west of the Qumran cliffs there had once been three small, walled towns. Nobody was stirred by this information for a long time, until after the discovery of the Dead Sea Scrolls. Then two scientists with the Palestinian Museum—American Frank Cross and Polish-born Father Joseph Milik—went out to the plain and found the ruins of all three towns. Evidence showed that the towns had been inhabited from about 850 B. C. to about 600 B. C. —from the time of Elijah to the invasion of the Babylonian King Nebuchadnezzar. Both men most likely passed this way. It was not far from here that Elijah departed on the flaming chariot. Evidence also showed that the sites had subsequently been briefly occupied—Roman coins, sherds, pottery like the pottery made at Qumran. Some graves were found, but all that was disclosed about them was that they resembled those at the monastery. This would mean that they were rectangular, between four and six feet deep. They would have been three abreast, with intermittent transverse paths, depending on the number. The floor would have been paved with brick. A layer of stone would have been placed over the body, like a covering, then the soil fill. The body would be on its back, its head to the south, with its hands either crossed at the pelvis or at its side. The age of the skeltons could be determined, but this was not given. If, however, they are as old as the towns themselves, then there would be grounds to assume that an Essenic-like people lived here on the plain as much as seven hundred years before the monastery was built. And this would give credence to the Edgar Cayce information, to the effect that Essenism was not a relatively new concept at the time of Jesus and that there had been plenty of time for it to spread out, in a variety of expressions, to all of the then known world.

Though there are numerous references to the Essenic and the Palestinian periods in the Cayce Readings, there are two Readings in which the information is particularly abundant. Both Readings were done for literary purposes. In both instances, follow-ups were done for three and four years. One was for the benefit of Tom Sugrue, Cayce's biographer. The other was for Case 2067, a middle-aged woman who was a professor at an Eastern college, and who also wrote. This was, in fact, the person to whom Cayce once sent a testy reprimand because the questions she sent him were so scattershot and entered areas which he felt were not his. The Reading contains a few examples of Cayce's mild impatience with the woman for expecting too much, but some of his gentle reprimand is good advice for anybody who writes. And this: the Reading contains a few instances where the information differs from what was given during other Readings but, as was established during Cayce's lifetime, this sometimes happened because of the way the question was phrased and at other times because the information was not available at the moment.

The woman's first Reading took place on December 22, 1939, and Cayce said:

"Before that the entity was in the land of the Master-of-masters' sojourn in the earth. During those periods the entity was a queen of no mean estate, and she took hold upon the words of the Master—though never personally coming in contact with Him. For the entity then was the companion or wife of Herod, who sought His destruction. Yet the entity's experience there, as Thesea, sought a closer comprehending of the Wise Men.

"Thus the entity will, or may, in this experience, find, even by the conversation with one of these that is in the city of its own birth, the interpretations of those experiences and periods that brought about the determinations to cry out, as it did, that brought material of physical extinction and bore in its activity the very same influences and forces that were upon the minds of many by Calvary. For as the entity reasoned with the Essenes, as well as conversed with the Wise Men who came with the new messages to the world, the entity proclaimed that pronouncement that He Himself then being announced had given: 'Others may do as they may; but as for me and my house, we will serve the living God.' Do not interpret this to mean those who may be in thine own physical household. Thy house is indeed thy body—*that* is the temple of the living God. *That* is the *whole* house made to conform to the will, the way: 'He that loves me keeps my commandments' in body, in mind, in soul.

"Through the experience the entity gained and the entity lost; yet these very happenings of that land were written by the entity—as to how there were the longings in the hearts of those peoples, especially from the days of the return to the Holy Land, through the provisions of those forces that were as in answer to a law, 'If ye call, I will hear, said the Lord of hosts.' Hence the entity wrote

143

concerning those peoples through those periods from the prophets to the period when the announcing had been to those groups who sought for His coming. And these were a part of the records as destroyed by her own children in the Alexandrian library, as well as in the 'city in the hills and the plains.'

"In those things again, then, the entity may find an outlet, by the conversation with and the recording of the experiences of self in the various activities as impelled people of different lands, different environs. And yet, as has been before indicated, know that the message is *one;* for the Lord thy God is one, and that Jesus *is* the one who was promised from that day: 'and her seed shall bruise his head.' In these manners may the entity in its writing, in its lecturing, in its service among its fellowmen, not merely induce and persuade but so present such as may arouse the individual souls to open their hearts to Him—who stands and knocks."

Almost a year later, on September 3, 1940, Cayce told the same woman:

"The entity was well acquainted with many of that group of the Essenes during that time, for the entity was a seeker not only for the unusual but for the mystical powers proclaimed by many of that group through those periods of activity. Then there came those periods of persecutions, for these were the attempts of the companion to court favors with the dictators or procurators who were in charge during those periods of the entity's experiences or activity. This, as indicated by the Scripture, brought some disturbing conditions with those of the Roman rule because of the changes that were very probable or that later came about, as to the emperors and their policies for handling those conditions and situations through the land. Thus the entity became acquainted with activities of a political and religious nature and the *general* relationships of the populace to those changing situations.

"When there were the orders for the destruction of the individuals, that their blood might be a portion of the sacrifice that was attempted, these brought abhorrence and the turning away from the close associations with the activities of the companion at the period. This brought great disturbances as to whys and wherefores of activities

144

by or through the divine interference or divine progress among men at the time. And these are a portion of the entity's own disturbing in the present, which have never, as to the entity, been completely answered. For there has not been the full understanding as to the meaning of the blood as shed for the eternal sacrifice or the law being of no effect in the law itself, that unless individuals, in body, in mind, in spirit, *become* the law it is then void in *their* experience—for they *are* the law. And the law is love, the law is God, the law *is* circumstances as experienced in the activities there.

"Through these periods the entity gained and lost— gained when self was put in the place of preserving or saving the individuals from special servitude and aiding in making it practical for the various groups to become more and more in accord with the tenets of some of the priests' activity and condemning the priests in their only making their office as a means for the gaining of material and social prestige. Thus it was not an easy life through the sojourn, for the entity was wedded when only fourteen, as would be termed today, and lived until the experiences of that announcement of the Christian or Christ experience."

The Reading on June 25, 1941, began with Gertrude Cayce stating: "You will have before you the material extracted from the Life Reading covering the period of Jesus' ministry and being prepared by 2067, present in this room, for pamphlet presentation. You will answer the questions which have been prepared for this work."

Cayce said: "Yes, we have the desires and the hopes, with the information that has been gathered. Ready for questions."

"Can you suggest an appropriate title for the Christ Ministry Pamphlet?"

"This depends much upon the manner in which the information is compiled—as to its purpose, as to its completeness and as to that it may accomplish. It would be best to leave this with those who would publish same."

Mrs. Cayce then read a list of subjects to be covered in the pamphlet, and she asked: "Would you include the major part of this material in one pamphlet or how would you suggest it be arranged?"

Cayce said: "*Again*—what is the purpose? What is to be gained from this that has not been accomplished in other data of similar nature? Is it for the propagation of propaganda for a group that is attempting to make a cult or is it to supply the needed stimuli to all for service in the channels in which they find themselves drawn for one cause or another? This depends, then, upon that phase of the approach, as to how or in what manner this would be prepared for distribution."

"Please suggest to the entity the purpose of the pamphlet and the especial timeliness of the pamphlet assigned to her."

Cayce seemed annoyed. "Why would you suggest a purpose for preparing a pamphlet when there has been indicated the purpose for which she is preparing same? This is superficial! This has to be reached before there is begun any actuality of preparation and followed with a purpose, with a desire. Such cannot be *prepared* for anyone. It has to be *sought*. Such data are prepared by those who give of themselves. Did the Father prepare the Master or did the Master prepare Himself for the Father's purpose? Then should the entity prepare herself for what she hopes to give to others or should what is to be given here prepare the entity?"

The questions took a different turn. "Why do historians like Josephus ignore the massacre of the infants and the history of Christ, when they record minute details of all other historical events?"

"What was the purpose of Josephus' writing? For the Jews or for the Christians? This answers itself."

"In one Reading we are told Jesus' birthday was on March 19 according to as we would reckon time now. In another Reading we were told that we keep Christmas about the right time, the twenty-fourth or twenty-fifth of December as we have our time now. Please explain seeming contradiction."

"Both are correct according to the time from which same were reckoned. How many times have there been the reckonings? Take these in consideration, with the period of events being followed in the information indicated. Just as there was the reckoning from the various groups for their individual activity, so was the informa-

146

tion given as to the records from that source with which those seeking were concerned."

"A Reading states that the historic events from the time of the prophets until Christ were written by Thesea, Herod's wife. Why did her children destroy these writings in the Alexandrian Library and are there any of these writings left on earth at the present time?"

"Her children did not destroy them. They were destroyed by the Mohammedans and the divisions in the church, who were the Jews and not the Romans nor the mixture of the Roman and Jewish influence. There are not these records, save as may be attained from some present in the Vatican."

"Was Jesus as a child also able to perform miracles, as the Catholic Church claims, and was he clairaudient, clairvoyant, and did He remember His past incarnations?"

"Read the first chapter of John and you will see. As to the activities of the child—the apparel brought more and more the influence which today would be called a lucky charm or a lucky chance, not as a consciousness. This (the consciousness) began with the ministry from that period when He sought the activities from the entrance in the temple and disputing or conversing with the rabbi at the age of twelve. Thus the seeking for the study through the associations with the teachers at that period."

"Is it true that Jesus in His youth loved Mary, Martha's sister, as a sweetheart or did He never have a sweetheart?"

"Mary, the sister of Martha, was a harlot—until the cleansing, and not one that Jesus would have loved, though He loved all. The closer associations brought to the physical or filial love were with the children and not with those the age of the Master."

"Please describe Jesus' education in India—schools attended. And did He attend the Essene school in Jagannath taught by Lamaas? Did He study in Benares also, under the Hindu teacher Udraka?"

"He was there at least three years. Arcahia was the teacher."

"Did He attend the schools in Jagannath?"

"*All* were a portion of the teachings as combined from the Essene schools, but these were not the true Essene doctrine as practiced by the Jewish and semi-Jewish associations in Carmel."

"Did He study in Benares also under the Hindu teacher Udraka?"

"Rather that as indicated—Arcahia."

"Please describe Jesus' education in Egypt in Essene schools of Alexandria and Heliopolis, naming some of His outstanding teachers and subjects studied."

"Not in Alexandria—rather in Heliopolis, for the periods of attaining to the priesthood or the taking of the examinations there, as did John. One was in one class, one in the other."

"Please describe Jesus' contact with schools in Persia, and did He at Persepolis establish a method of entering the Silence as well as demonstrating healing power?"

"Rather that was a portion of the activity in the 'city in the hills and the plains.' "

"Name some of His outstanding teachers and subjects studied."

"Not as teachers, but as being *examined* by these, passing the tests there. These, as they have been since their establishing, were tests through which one attained to that place of being accepted or rejected by the influences of the mystics as well as of the various groups or schools in other lands. For, as indicated oft through this channel, the unifying of the teachings of many lands was brought together in Egypt, for that was the center from which there was to be the radial activity of influence in the earth—as indicated by the first establishing of those tests or the recording of time as it has been, was and is to be, until the new cycle is begun."

"Why does not the Bible tell of Jesus' education or are there manuscripts now on earth that will give these missing details to be found soon?"

"There are some that have been forged manuscripts. All of those that existed were destroyed—that is, the originals—with the activities in Alexandria."

"Did Lazaraus visit other planets and spiritual realms the four days his body lay in the tomb before Jesus raised him?"

Cayce cleared his throat, impatiently. "We haven't Lazarus here today!"

"Can you tell of angels and visions and dreams that strengthened Jesus, other than those mentioned in the Bible?"

"If there will be recorded those signified by the periods of separation as indicated there (in the Bible), we will have sufficient for verification of this strengthening throughout His *whole* ministry, for these occur at regular periods."

"When did the knowledge come to Jesus that He was to be the Savior of the world?"

"When He fell in Eden."

"Can you give the name of the lad who furnished the five loaves and two fishes at the feeding of the five thousand?"

"We may supply same, but not from here."

"Did Jesus study under Apollo and other Greek philosophers and was it through educational contacts that the Greeks later came to Him to beg Him to come to their country when the Jews cast Him out?"

"We do not find such. Jesus, as Jesus, never appealed to the wordly-wise."

"Please explain more about Mary being the twin soul of Jesus and her refusal to reincarnate, and her deity?"

"We do not find such as even being true." (This was in answer to the entire question.)

Then: "In one Reading we are told the Wise Men came from India, Egypt and Gobi; in another Reading we are told the Wise Men who brought the incense came from Persia. Which is correct? And besides the Wise Men Achlar and Ashtueil, what were the names of the other two Wise Men?"

"Both are correct. There was more than one visit of the Wise Men. One is a record of three Wise Men. There was a fourth, as well as the fifth, and then the second group. They came from Persia, India, Egypt, and also from Chaldea, Gobi, and what is *now* the 'Indo' or 'Tao' land." (Indochina.)

"A Reading gives Sylvia as a man stoned with Stephen and Anniaus as a woman of the household of Cyrenius. Are these names correct?"

"Correct."

"Teleman, in a Reading, was reported as being of the

household where Philemon was a servant. Is that the same Philemon whose servant Paul sent back?"

"Same Philemon."

"Was Judas Iscariot's idea in betraying Jesus to force Him to assert Himself as a King and bring in His Kingdom then?"

"Rather the *desire* of the man to force same, and the fulfilling of that as Jesus spoke of same at the supper."

"Is Herod the Great now on earth and will he be located through the Readings?"

"We haven't Herod the Great."

"Were Mary and Elizabeth taught in a sacred grove in Egypt for a time by teachers, Elihus and Salome, that they might better instruct their sons, Jesus and John?"

"We don't find this to be true. Their education was rather with those headed by the Essenes, through which Zachariah was called as the one to and through whom would come those influences as became the forerunner of the Christ. These were rather in the Palestine land. They were in the Holy Land, and at Mount Moriah."

"Please describe Jesus' initiations in Egypt, telling if the Gospel reference to three days and nights in the grave or tomb, possibly in the shape of a cross, indicates a special initiation."

"This is a portion of the initiation. It is part of the passage through that (experience) to which each soul is to attain in its development, as has the world through each period of their incarnation in the earth. As is supposed, the record of the earth through the passage through the tomb—or pyramid—is that through which each entity, each soul, as an initiate, must pass for the attaining to the releasing of same—as indicated by the empty tomb, which has *never* been filled, see? Only Jesus was able to break same, as it became that which indicated His fulfillment. And then, as the initiate, He went out for the passing through the initiation by fulfilling, as indicated in the baptism in the Jordan—not standing in it and being poured or sprinkled either—as He passed from that activity into the wilderness to meet that which had been His undoing in the beginning."

Two years later, the woman was still working on the

150

pamphlet, and on February 22, 1943, another Reading was held, this one conducted by Hugh Lynn Cayce, and the first question was: "For the title of the Christ Ministry book, will 'Jesus, The Essene' be acceptable?"

"It would be to some, but to more it would not."

"Would you suggest a suitable title?"

"Who's writing the book?" Cayce asked, again impatient. "From here? Or from the compilations? It would be preferable that the data be *prepared,* and then *from* that there may be indicated the better title. 'The Early Ministry' or 'The Early Life' or 'The Life of Jesus As The Essene,' not 'Jesus, The Essene.' "

"For literary purposes, please describe a secret Essene meeting before Christ, at which Judy or her parents or Thesea or some Bible characters were present."

"This might be described very well as by any authentic meeting of certain groups founded by Solomon. But the description should not be from here, for it would be quite at variance to much of the data prepared. Draw upon thy own imagination. The Essenes were a group of individuals sincere in their purpose, and yet not orthodox as to the rabbis of that particular period. Thus such a meeting would be described by the meditations, certain ritualistic formulas, as may be outlined very well from some of those activities as may be gathered from the activities of the priest in the early period when there was the establishing of the tabernacle. Remember, recall, the first two didn't do so well, even under the direction of the high priest, for they offered strange fire. Let not, then, that as would be offered here become as strange fire, but as in keeping with the precept of Jesus, 'I and the Father are one'—not individually but in the personal application of the tenets, commandments, being one in purpose, one in application. Thus such a meeting would be the interpreting of each promise that has been made, as to when, as to how, there would come the Promised One. Analyze in the mind, then, that from the third of Genesis through to the last, even, of Malachi. Set them aside. Use them as the basis of discussions, as the various groups may be set in order, each rotating as a teacher, as an instructor, for that particular meeting, remembering all were secret meetings."

"Tell of the work, the prophecies, the hopes of Phinehas and Elkatma, Judy's parents, at Carmel, as Essenes."

"These were those activities that may be illustrated very well in the ministry of the parents of the strong man, that a parallel may be drawn as to how first there was the appearance to the mother and then the father, as to what should be the ministry, the activity, of the entity that was to lead that group and aid in the early teaching of the prophecies of the life of the child Jesus, as well as of John. For John was more the Essene than Jesus. Jesus held rather to the spirit of the law and John to the letter of same."

"Was Judy immaculately conceived, as perhaps Samuel was?"

"Neither was immaculately conceived."

"In Jewish history, was anybody but Mary and Jesus immaculately conceived?"

"Mary was not immaculately conceived. Jesus was. There have been others, but not in Jewish history." (This conflicts with other Readings on Mary, and Cayce did not explain it.)

"Why was Judy not a boy as expected?"

"This is from the powers on high and gave the first demonstration of woman's place in the affairs and associations of man. For, as were the teachings of Jesus, it released woman from that bondage to which she had been held by the ideas of man conceived from the fall of Eve or of woman's first acceptance of the ideas. These were the first, and those activities it brought about, in the teachings materially, were as Jesus proclaimed."

"For what purpose was Judy sent into the world at that time?"

"Just indicated."

"Describe any outstanding points or unusual abilities Judy had."

"Only as one brought into those activities: it may well be described as the feminine of Samson."

"Where did Judy receive her education, in what subjects, and who were her teachers?"

"The Holy Spirit, and the mother and father; not from other sources, though there were those activities from all of the teachings of the East, through those early

152

periods before there were those acceptances of Judy as the leader of the Essenes at Carmel at that period."

"During the life time of Jesus, where did Judy live and with whom?"

"In Carmel, with the companion and the mother."

"Please describe Judy's personal appearance, her dress, her personality, her faith."

"Draw upon the imagination for these. As would be the dress of Samson, making it feminine."

"Tell of Judy's marriage, the name of her husband, his work, names of children and their accomplishments."

"His work had to do with the records that were translated for the various groups. The activities of Judy through these experiences were much as might be termed those of Hannah, during those periods when there were those seekings for that from the Lord that might give a recompense for those doubts brought by others."

"What were the names of Judy's children?"

Impatience again. "These have little to do with that needed. This has been indicated."

"What were the 'fears' that wrecked Judy's son who is now (Case 2795), and why was Judy, the healer, unable to heal him?"

"It was not disease, other than that within self. Why were Samuel's sons sinners? These may only be answered within the individual or from the seeking of the individual himself."

"Tell about the angels appearing to Judy, when, where, and what they said."

"Which period? These were many and oft."

"Please describe Judy's home life as well as her Essene activities."

"That as might be the description of an individual who had set self aside as a channel for such activities. These are very hard to be understood from the material mind—or from the material understanding or concept, especially in this period of consciousness. For then man walked close with God, when there were those preparations—it is possible in the present but not *acceptable.* Consequently, to describe the home life as to say they sat in the sun, ate three square meals a day and wore little or nothing or that they dressed in the

153

best—it must be that as from the spirit. May best be described as given by Luke, in his description of those things that disturbed Mary. 'She kept these things and pondered them in her heart.' This did not prevent her from being, then, a material person, nor one with the faculties and desires for material associations—as indicated in the lack of celibacy. Is this indicated in any condition in the book? Or man's relationship to God? Nowhere is this indicated!"

"Tell about Judy teaching Jesus, where and what subjects she taught Him, and what subjects she planned to have Him study abroad."

"The prophecies! Where? In her home. When? During those periods from his twelfth to his fifteenth-sixteenth year, when He went to Persia and then to India. In Persia, when His 'father' died. In India when John went first to Egypt, where Jesus joined him and both became the initiates in the pyramid or temple there."

"What subjects did Judy plan to have Him study abroad?"

"What you would today call astrology."

"At what major events in Jesus' life was Judy present —as at casting out of demons, healing, feeding the five thousand, and so on?"

"At His teaching, for a period of some five years."

"Was she present at any of the healings or the feeding of the multitudes?"

"Those where she chose to, but she was very old then. She lived to be sufficiently old to know, of course, of the feeding of the first five thousand. She was present, but rather as one that brought the crowds together than as contributing to the activities at the time. For there the divisions arose, to be sure."

"Was Judy present at the Crucifixion or the Resurrection?"

"No. In spirit—that is, in mind—present. For, remember, Judy's experience at that time was such that she might be present in many places without the physical body being there."

"Tell of instances when Judy and Thesea, the Essene, worked or planned together."

"Only at the regular periods or meeting of the Essenes,

154

as we find." Cayce paused, then said: "We are covering too great a period here. Draw something on the self! We are through for the present."

Edgar Cayce and Tom Sugrue first met in 1927, and, for both, the meeting was the beginning of a lifelong friendship. A writer and an editor, Sugrue's primary interest in Cayce was professional; but as they became friends, Sugrue developed a deep interest in Cayce's work as well as his life and he became an avid student of the Readings. Though Sugrue did other writings about Cayce he waited twenty-five years before publishing the biography. He spent summers at Virginia Beach; when he went seriously to work on the biography, he was a guest in the Cayce home for almost two years. His research was often done by Readings, as he sought understanding of the Caycean philosophy, and some of the information that was given pertained to the Essenic movement. For example, on June 27, 1937, the discussion turned to the circumstances of the birth of Jesus, and Cayce said:

"Much might be given as to how or why and when there were the purposes that brought about the materialization of Jesus in the flesh. In giving then the history: There were those in the faith of the fathers to whom the promises were given that these would be fulfilled as from the beginning of man's record. Hence there was the continued preparation and dedication of those who might be the channels through which this chosen vessel might enter—through choice—into materiality. Thus in Carmel, where there were the priests of this faith, there were the maidens chosen that were dedicated to this purpose, this office, this service. Among them was Mary, the beloved, the chosen one, and she, as had been foretold, was chosen as the channel. Thus she was separated and kept in the closer association with and in the care or charge of this office. That was the beginning, that was the foundation, of what ye term the Church.

"Then, when the days were fulfilled that the prophecy might come that had been given by Isaiah, Malachi, Joel and those of old, she—Mary—espoused of Joseph, a chosen vessel for the office among those of the priests— the sect or group—who had separated and dedicated themselves in body, in mind, in spirit, for this coming, became with child. Then, as the record is given, that is common knowledge to most, there was born in Bethlehem of Judea that entity, that soul, Jesus. There was the period of purification according to the law, and then the days in the temple and the blessing by Anna and by the high priest.

"And these made for those days of the beginning of the entity called Jesus—who becomes the Christ, the Master of Masters—in the days when there was the return to Nazareth and then the edict that sent them into Egypt so that the prophecy can be fulfilled, 'My son shall be called from Egypt.' There five years were spent, as ye term time, by the mother, Joseph and the Child. Then there was the return to Judea and to Capernaum, where dwelt many of those who were later the closer companions of the Master.

"Here, after the period again of presentation at the temple, when there were those questionings among the groups of the leaders, the entity was sent first—again—into Egypt for only a short period, and then into India, and then into what is now Persia. Hence in all the ways of the teachers the entity was trained. From Persia He was called to Judea at the death of Joseph, and then into Egypt for the completion of the preparation as a teacher. He was with John, the messenger, during the portion of the training there in Egypt. Then to Capernaum, Cana, and those periods of the first preparation in the land of the nativity. The rest ye have according to Mark, John, Matthew and Luke. These in their order record most of the material experiences of the Master. Many of details may be given in the varied fields of the preparation, but these were the experiences. Ready for questions."

Through Gertrude Cayce, Sugrue asked: "Explain the immaculate conception."

Cayce said: "As becoming flesh is the activity of the mental being (or the spiritual self and mental being) pushing itself into matter; and as spirit—as He gave— is neither male nor female, they are then both—or one. Thus the immaculate conception is the physical and mental so attuned to spirit as to be quickened by same. Hence the spirit, the soul, of the Master then was brought

156

into being through the accord of the Mother in materiality that ye know in the earth as conception:"

"Explain the relationship of the Wise Men and Jesus' birth."

"As indicated by the travels of the Master during the periods of preparation, the whole earth, the whole world, looked for, sought, the closer understanding. Hence through the efforts of the students of the various phases of experiences of men in the earth, as may be literally interpreted from the first chapters of Genesis, ye find that those that subdued—not that were ruled by but subdued—the understanding of that in the earth were considered or were in the position of the wise or the sages or the ones that were holy—in body and mind, in accord with purposes.

"Hence we find the Wise Men as those that were seekers for the truth, for this 'happening,' and in and through the application of those forces—as ye would term today 'psychic'—we find them coming to the place where the child was. Or they were drawn as those that were giving the thanks for this Gift, this expression of a soul seeking to show wayward man back to God. So they represent in the metaphysical sense the three phases of man's experience in materiality: gold, the material; frankincense, the ether or ethereal; myrrh, the healing force as brought by same—thus body, mind, soul.

"These were the positions, then, of the Wise men in their relationship. Or to put into the parlance of the day: they were the encouragement needed for the Mother and those that had nourished, that had cherished, this event in the experience of mankind. They came during the days of purification, but to be sure only after she was purified were they presented to the Child."

"What relation did they have with the later travels of Jesus?"

"As has just been indicated, they represented then the three phases of man's experience as well as the three phases of the teacher from Egypt, from Persia, from India."

"Did Mary and Joseph have any other children?"

"James, Jude and the daughter."

157

"Does the immaculate conception, as explained, concern the coming of Mary to Anne or Jesus to Mary?"

"Of Jesus to Mary."

"Was Mary immaculately conceived?"

"Mary was immaculately conceived."

"How long was the preparation in progress before Mary was chosen?"

"Three years."

"In what manner was she chosen?"

"As they walked up the steps."

"Was there any appearance of the angel Gabriel in the home?"

"In the temple, when she was chosen; in the home of Elizabeth, when she was made aware of the 'presence' by again being in the presence of the messenger or forerunner. Again to Joseph at the time of their union. Again —by Michael—at the time when the edict was given."

On June 22, 1941, Sugrue requested further information on the circumstances of the birth of Jesus and the marriage at Cana. As will be shown in the next chapter, other Readings touch on these events in different and dramatic detail. For now, Cayce said this about Bethlehem:

"The purposes are well known, for which the journey was made in the period. The activities of Joseph are well known. The variation or difference in their ages is not so oft dwelt upon. Neither is there much indicated in sacred or profane history as to the preparation of the mother for that channel through which immaculate conception might take place. And this, the immaculate conception, is a stumblingstone to many wordly-wise.

"The arrival was in the evening—not as counted from the Roman time, not that declared to Moses by God when the second passover was to be kept, not that same time which was in common usage even in that land—but what would *now* represent January sixth. The weather was cool, and there were crowds on the way, for it was only a sabbath day's journey from Jerusalem. There were great crowds of people on the way from the hills of Judea.

"The people were active in the occupations of the varied natures in that unusual land. Some were carpenters,

158

as those of the house of Joseph, who had been delayed, even on the journey, by the condition of the Mother. Some in the group were helpers to Joseph—carpenters' helpers. Then there were shepherds, husbandmen, and the varied groups that had their small surroundings as necessitated by the conditions of the fields about Nazareth.

"In the evening, then, or at twilight, Joseph approached the inn, which was filled with those who had also journeyed there on their way to be polled for the tax as imposed by the Romans upon the people of the land, for those had been sent out who were to judge the abilities of the varied groups to be taxed. And each individual was required by the Roman law to be polled in the city of his birth. Both Joseph and Mary were members of the sect called the Essenes, and thus they were questioned by those not only in the political but in the religious authority in the cities.

"Then there was the answer by the innkeeper, 'No room in the inn,' especially for such an occasion. Laughter and jeers followed, at the sight of the elderly man with the beautiful girl, his wife, heavy with child. Disappointments were written upon not only the face of Joseph but the innkeeper's daughter, as well as those of certain groups about the inn, for many saw the possibilities of an unusual story that might be gained if the birth were to take place in the inn. Also there was consternation outside, among those who had heard that Joseph and Mary had arrived and were not given a room. They began to seek some place, some shelter. Remember, many of these, too, were of that questioned group, who had heard of that girl, that lovely wife of Joseph who had been chosen by the angels on the stair, who had heard of what had taken place in the hills where Elizabeth had gone, when there was the visit from the cousin, and as to those things which had also come to pass in her experience. Such stories were whispered from one to another. Thus many joined in the search for some place. Necessity demanded that some place be sought—quickly. Then it was found, under the hill, in the stable, above which the shepherds were gathering their flocks into the field.

"There the Savior, the Child, was born who, through

159

the will and the life manifested, became the Savior of
the world, that channel through which those of old had
been told that the promise would be fulfilled that was
made to Eve, the arising again of another like unto
Moses and, as given to David, the promise was not to
depart from that channel. But lower and lower man's
concept of needs had fallen. Then, when hope seemed
gone, the herald angels sang. The star appeared that made
the wonderment to the shepherds, that caused the awe
and consternation to all of those about the inn, some
making fun, some smitten with conviction that those unkind things said must needs be readjusted in their relationships to things coming to pass. All were in awe as
the brightness of His star appeared and shone, as the
music of the spheres brought that joyful choir: *'Peace on
earth! Good will to men of good faith.'*

"All felt the vibrations and saw a great light—not
only the shepherds above the stable but those in the
inn as well. To be sure, those conditions were later to
be dispelled by the doubters, who told people that they
had been overcome with wine or what not.

"Just as the midnight hour came, there was the birth
of the Master. The daughter of the innkeeper was soon
upon the scene, as was the mother of the daughter, and
the shepherds that answered the cry and had gone to
see what was come to pass. These were the manners and
the ones present soon afterwards. Through the period
of purification the Mother remained there, not deeming
it best to leave, though all forms of assistance were
offered, not leaving until there was the circumcision and
the presenting in the temple to the magi, to Anna and
to Simeon. Such were the surroundings at the period of
the birth of Jesus."

Edgar Cayce said this about Cana:

"A great deal of that leading to the experience, to be
sure, is being skipped over, for that came about soon
after the return of the Master from the Jordan and
His dwelling by the sea, His conversation with Peter,
after Andrew had told Peter of the happenings at the
Jordan, and there was the wedding in Cana of Galilee.

"The girl was a relative of those close to the Mother
of Jesus, who prepared the wedding feast—as was

the custom in that period and is yet among those of the
Jewish faith who adhere to the traditions as well as the
custom of those people chosen as the channel because of
their purpose with God. The girl to be wed was a daughter
of the cousin of Mary, a daughter of a younger sister
of Elizabeth, whose name was also Mary. And she was
the one spoke of as 'the other Mary,' and not as some
have supposed.

"The customs required that there be a feast, which was
composed of the roasted lamb with the herbs, the breads
that had been prepared in the special ways as were the
custom and tradition of those who followed close to the
faith in Moses' law, Moses' custom, Moses' ordinances.
The families of Mary were present, as well as those of
the groom. The groom, in the name Roael, was among
the sons of Zebedee, being an older brother of James
and John who later became close followers of Jesus.

"The Master, returning with those who were hangers-
on, naturally sought to speak with His mother. Learning
of this happening, He, too, with the followers, were bid
to remain at the feast. Much wine also was part of the
custom. The day was what ye would call June third.
There were plenty of flowers and things of the field, yet
only a part of those things needed, for the custom called
for more of the meats prepared with certain herbs and
for wines. The day had been fine; the evening was fair; the
moon was full. This then brought the activities with
the imbibing more and more of wine, more hilarity, and
the dance which was in the form of the circles that were
a part of the customs not only of that land then but
that are in your own land now and then being revived.
With these activities, as indicated, the wine ran low. Remember, the sons of Zebedee were among those of the
upper class, as would be termed, not the poorer ones.
Thence the reason why Mary served or prepared for the
relative the feast.

"From those happenings that were a portion of her
experience upon their return from Egypt—as to how the
increase had come in the food when they had been
turned aside as they journeyed back towards the Promised Land—Mary felt, knew, was convinced within herself, that here again there might be such an experience,

161

with her son now returning as a man starting upon His mission. For, what was the pronouncement to the mother when Gabriel spoke to Her? What was the happening with Elizabeth when the mother spoke to her?

"This might be called a first period of test, for had He not just ten days ago sent Satan away and received ministry from the angels? This had come to be known as hearsay. Hence the natural questioning of the mother-love for the purposes. This son, strange in many ways, had chosen, by the dwelling in the wilderness for the forty days and then the returning to the lowly people, the fishermen from about the country. It brought on the questioning by the mother."

And the mission began with a miracle.

NINE

The Edgar Cayce Readings give the impression that there was scarcely a moment of Jesus' life that went untouched by Essenic influences from the first moment of that life. A pattern evolves which suggests that by their own psychic faculties they not only had foreknowledge of the arrival of the Christus but they were also aware of the dangers which would surround His life. Apparently these dangers existed even before Herod's edict. On June 23, 1936, while doing a second Life Reading on a man of fifty-eight, Cayce told him:

"Before that we find the entity was among those who came under the activities during those experiences when the Master walked in the land of promise. For the entity lived in the days when there were the preparations for the activities of the Master, many of which were in the hands, as it were, of the entity, because the entity then was that man, the keeper of the inn, to which Joseph made application for a place for the birth of the Master of men. Much of that as has been recorded as we find is not so well, nor in keeping with what the entity did then, as Apsafar, who was of the Essenes, though of a Jewish descent, though a combination of the Jewish and the Grecian. For the entity then made a study of those peoples, knew of those things that had been foretold by the teachers of the Essenes, and made all preparations as near in keeping with which had been foretold as possible.

"While among the entity's stables was indeed the place of rest, it was because of the very *rabble,* the very act of those that were in authority—both as to the Roman as well as the various groups—that were, in their discussions, making for the very things that would hinder or prevent those experiences that had been foretold. The entity did this rather for protection than because—as has been said—there was 'no room in the inn.' But this was meant to be implied, or conveyed, that they had been turned away. Yet in the entity's activities it was really for the protection. For the entity, too, had seen a vision; the entity, too, had heard, had known, of the voices that were in the air. The entity, too, had seen the star in the east. The entity, too, had known of those experiences that must befall those that were making all the preparations possible under those existent conditions for Him that should come as a teacher, as a shepherd, as a savior.

"Hence the experiences of the entity were as of those that are ever present in the entity's inner self. And when there is sorrow, when there are cares for others, these become rather as an appealing experience in the entity's activities. These are innate and are built from those experiences in that land about Bethany, in which the great development, the great experiences, came. For the entity was in that position where it stood rather not as one that made for a spy, either upon the Jewish or the Roman or those of its own peoples, but rather as a counsellor to those that sought to overcome those oppressions that were of a political as well as of a religious nature, owing to those conditions existing between the Pharisees, the Sadducees, the Essenes, the Romans and those teachings that were gradually being presented from the Grecians—or the entity's peoples—for the correlation of the philosophies that were of the Grecians and those activities with the Teacher, the Nazarene.

"Hence the entity, though in years, came to know the experiences, and there did the entity knows its present companion or wife. Their relationships then were rather as father and daughter in the experience, for she *stood* watch. In the experience, then, there comes in from those activities the very nature of the religious influence, but the adherence to any particular sect or any particular denomination, as ye term, or any particular group, seems to have a drawback to the entity because of those very experiences of contentions that arose during that sojourn.

"First know thine own ideal, as thou didst find in thine studies as the innkeeper upon the gateway to the city of learning. As thou didst keep in touch with those from Carmel's gates, so in thy dealings with thy fellow man in every walk of life thou mayest become as the gateway to understanding for many. Yet carry with these the basic forces as make for that as ye heard in thy declining years in the Bethany land, for thou wert present when he was raised from the dead, the friend Lazarus, as well as a friend to those that suffered through the experiences and the oppressions of those in authority."

This man's wife, who had been his daughter at the first Christmas, had the remarkable experience at that time of being the second person to hold the Infant Jesus. The midwife had been first, and then she passed the baby to this girl while attending to Mary. The daughter kissed the baby on the forehead. As was probably the case with most Essenes who lived outside the monastic communities, the information which this girl acquired about Jesus over the next thirty years came mostly over the grapevine; but when He began His ministry, she was one of the first to join Him. She was among the women who consoled Mary at the time of the Crucifixion and she became one of the first martyrs.

The Life Readings of Case 1151, who was a man of forty-eight when he began to consult Cayce in 1937, offer a uniquely broader view of events of those times. Cayce told him:

"It was in those years when there was the establishing

164

of the Julian calendar and when changes were wrought as to times. Hence the record will be measured here from that in which time was counted later. In that portion of the land now called Rome, then a portion of Heliopolis, the entity was the son then of one Antonius and Josie and came in the activities of the Roman experience, educated in the ways of those people that were both for the Roman and the Grecian forces. And those things that became a part of the experiences were the lessons which had been taught by the Grecian soldier that later fed the hemlock. Thus the entity grew into grace with those in authority, through the activities as came under the influences of Caesar Augustus, later Claudius and those that ruled over the varied lands that had become a portion of the experiences—or under the direction of the Romans.

"The entity, as has been indicated, was one who traveled through those lands, making those associations, those recommendations, for the manners in which the peoples under the various schools would be taxed, according to their *spiritual* counsel—or according to what ye would call the religious influences and the judging of these. Hence we find the man, then, at thirty, coming into associations during those periods when the Master walked in the earth as the young man just beginning the ministry.

"In these associations the entity came in close contact with those of the household from which the Master had gone out, becoming associated with, later married to (and by the Master), the *sister* of the Master—the *only* sister, who had received education in Greece and Rome through the associations of the family with the sects of the Jews and a portion that favored the Romans.

"Hence much of that which had been a portion of the experience of the household of Mary and Joseph was known to the entity. And when the Master was called home, owing to the death of Joseph, the husband of Mary, the entity then first became the closer associated with Jesus, the Master. For owing to the visitations of Jesus to men in other lands, and because of the Roman rule and the changes wrought, the entity—then Romacio

165

—found it necessary to make for the activities that brought a closer understanding.

"During those periods the activities were in keeping the Jewish masters or the Jewish rulers *coordinating* with the activities of the Roman rulers—as in that particular province in which the greater activities were under Pontius Pilate. Hence we find, as would be applied in the present, as is the experience of the entity ever in the present experience, the entity became as one associated with the producer and that produced—or with the capital and the labor or the activities as related to same. These become a natural activity from same; as then many of not only the tax assessors, the tax gatherers but those who judged in the various provinces as to the amounts, as to the abilities, came under the supervision of the entity during those experiences.

"Hence we find there were many of those that were the followers, yea, the disciples, later called Apostles, who became close friends then in one manner or another of the entity.

"It is sometimes judged that most of the disciples were poor, and this was not true. For Zebedee and his sons and Matthew the publican, all of whom were closely associated, were rather well-to-do. Peter and Andrew, of course, were servants or laborers with the sons of Zebedee; but Zebedee was among the wealthy and among those closely associated with those in authority. For as these were a portion of the family of which John, James, Jude, Ruth and all became a part, these were kinsmen and were people that were in authority so far as capital is concerned, as ye would term in the present, and were not poor. While Peter, Andrew, Thomas, Alphaeus were not of the wealthy, all of these were known to the entity, as also was Matthew, as just given, who had been one appointed by an aide of the entity in the experience.

"Thus came the closer understanding. For the entity then studied, as it were, those things that *prompted* the activity of the various sets and sects—the Pharisees, the Sadducees, the Essenes, the influence upon the Roman soldiery as well as the Roman rule, as well as upon the individuals who were set in authority in the varied provinces.

"Then the period arrives when the entity is just called to Rome, during that period of the trial or just before the trial, during the Crucifixion, returning to Jerusalem or to those environs of same just the day *after* this had occurred. Thus we find the walk to Emmaus with the disciples, one Luke, the beloved physician, who was both a Roman and a Jew and *of* those same provinces in the Grecian rule that were under the Roman authorities. Thus we find the entity again *physically* in association, in touch with, the influence of the Master, Jesus, who became the Christ in the life lived.

"Thus we find the entity later, when there was the recall of Pilate because of that which had been brought about, returned to Rome as one who counseled with the Caesars for those very activities and making the changes that brought Philip and Agrippa and the judges that were to judge later when those periods in which Paul, Peter, John, Philip and Stephen were alive. These all became a portion of the experiences of the entity.

"Though remaining a Roman, the entity was in sympathy with those activities, lending counsel and giving those influences that prevented the full destruction of the disciples during those periods of experience. Is there any wonderment, then, that the entity in the present experience finds the urge for service? For it was gained by those close walks with the entity, the man, Jesus, who had given, 'He that would be the greatest among you, he is the servant of all.' These became, then, as it were, the sign, the guide, the directing influence in the experience of the entity. And we find little in that sojourn, that activity, that may be said to have been even a tendency towards retardment. For *all* was in purpose, in desire, to be even as He had taught, that they who for any cause lord over their fellow man become that as must sooner or later become a stumblingstone.

"And, as He gave also, each and every individual is in that position, that phase, that state of development or *unfoldment*, that they have builded in their application of that as He gave *is* the whole law: to love the Lord thy God with all thy body, thy mind, thy soul, and thy neighbor as thyself. This is the whole law. May all learn, as the entity strove then to apply those tenets, those

167

truths, in the *experiences* of those that were put in authority by man, yea, but that they might have, they might show, in their opportunity that the love of the Father surpasses the *glory* of man.

"Thus we find throughout the entity's experience and the entity's associations with those of what ye call or term the Palestine experience there was *no rebellion of* those peoples of the land against *Roman* authority. The rebellion came after those periods, when the entity was recalled to Rome or attempted to keep closer in touch with those who had been called to Rome for the questioning, such as was Paul who, by his own *self,* had brought misinterpreting, misunderstanding; as did Peter and the Church, even John. Here the entity, in the last acts of his intervention, *saved* that entity (John)—for the followers, for the world—from that death as the others had drawn or had come to. Hence the banishment of John was by the very *direct* intervention of the entity with those in authority, and the taking away from the churches that had been established in the various places that there might be preserved the records, for same also became a portion of the entity's experience.

"There was the passing, then, from the physical activity in Rome during that period when there were just the beginnings of the attempts for the unification of the religious as well as the penal laws or the laws in other lands ruled by the Roman empire. The entity once, just before the interventions, went to the libraries in Alexandria, and there were the attempts to placate any of the destructions that later became the loss to what is now called the Christian world. The entity was at that age or period some sixty years *after* the Crucifixion—then ninety years or ninety-three years of age at the passing."

The man had some questions. "I would like to know a more complete account of the report I made to Rome concerning the Christian movement in Palestine."

Cayce said: "These were of such varied characters that we find it necessary that all of these be taken as what may be termed individual reports, see? At the time when there was the recalling of Pilate and the reports that had been made as to the activities of the wife of Pilate as related to the healing that had been accomplished in the

168

household, then we find a very *favorable* report to the Christians, though the entity was questioned much by those who were directly under the supervision of the entity. But the report was accepted by the Roman emperor and acted upon according to the directions of the entity: that Pilate be removed and one closer in association or in sympathy with the Christian movement be appointed in the stead, as is seen or is recorded by profane history as well as by intimation in sacred history.

"During those periods when there were the uprisings, as in some places and positions, we find the reports then were not so severe against the individual activities of the Romans in authority, for never again do we find, as has just been given, any of the Roman *rulers* of the various provinces acting *without* the direction from Rome through the activities of the entity. While these reports were not that Rome should just *accept* the authority but that there be the *reasoning together*. For he gave then, as did the great teacher from the Sanhedrin—Gamaliel: let not ye find thyselves fighting against God. This might be said, then, to be the whole of the report. Not be in that attitude of condemning but do not act in such measures as to find thyself fighting against providence and God."

The man: "Did I secure information from the entity then known as Judy?"

"Information respecting the activities of the Essenes as to whether they were averse to the authority of the Jewish rulers as well as the Romans. The activities or lessons or information gained from the keeper of the records of the Essenes—or Judy—were those things that prompted the entity later to investigate for self those records that were reported to have been made and that were in the library at Alexandria, about the Wise Men that came from the other lands just before the birth and at the time of the birth presented themselves—or a few days later—in the town of Bethlehem. Yes, the entity gained—or obtained—a record of that as had been gathered by the keeper of records from Carmel."

The man: "How close a relationship had I with the entity known as Judy?"

"Just as would be intimated—as here the entity Judy

169

was held in reverence by all of the followers of Jesus, though persecuted oft by the Jews or the sects of the Jews—under various circumstances. But not as an informer was Judy considered by the entity, but as one that would and that did give the facts of the activities of various groups in respect to not only the Essenes but the other portions of the various groups in the land. The association then was quite close at times; at others not so closely associated yet keeping in touch with the activities."

The man: "Any advice that may be given at this time that will be of benefit and help?"

"Hold to that purpose that prompted thee not only in thy activities then but in those that ye are repeating in this experience, from those great awakenings and unfoldments that came to thee when thou had indeed learned, thou had experienced, indeed, 'I am my brother's keeper!'—even as the Master gave of His whole self— body and mind—risking even the spirit, that man might know there is an advocate with the Father. So can ye bring into the hearts and minds of those in authority, here or there, whether it be those that labor day by day or those that work in the office or wherever, the realization that *all* must work as the cog, the wheel, that must bring together all for *one* purpose—*service*, that the Father may be manifested through the love each soul shows for the other."

On April 26, 1934, a woman of thirty was given this information:

"Before that we find the entity was in that known as the Promised Land, during those periods when the Master walked in the earth. The entity then was among those that came under those influences in the sojourns of the Master in that land of Galilee, for the entity was then a daughter of Zebedee and a sister to those that were close in the activities of the Master in that land. Through that experience the entity gained in soul-development. While fears and doubts arose at times from the activities through the periods of persecution, that sojourn has builded and does make for those abilities to arouse in others those things that may be helpful in their mental and physical self; also that purposefulness in the inmost

170

self that may bring to the entity those satisfying things that bring joy, peace and harmony. And oft in the visions have there come periods when the entity has walked close with those during that sojourn."

Over the next three years, checks were made on this Reading—No. 540—and it was the check on February 20, 1936, that was particularly illuminating. By then, it had been established that the entity's name during the Palestinian Period had been Naomi and that she had been the sister of the Apostles James and John. Then Cayce told her:

"In giving the interpretation of that as we find here, do not let same become confusing because of customs of the surroundings, of the changes that are wrought in using the language of the present to describe that used or in use during the period of the entity's experience in the Palestine land. As we find here, in giving these descriptions, these are as those that made impressions, as it were, upon the skein of time and space. Hence they may be often viewed by others who may turn to such from a different angle. Yet that which may become the more worthwhile to the entity in making application of the experience and the effect made upon the soul of the entity by that which the entity may *experience* itself as it reviews same is what is being given. And it may become a part of the mental forces that *are* the builders in practical application of an experience upon an individual entity.

"Thus we find the entity was the daughter of Zebedee and the other Mary. These individuals were not of the rabble, not of the political, not of great *spiritual* influence or force among the associates of the group. While both were of the Jewish faith, as would be termed today, or the Hebraic faith, they were in that position socially which was above that of the ordinary individuals. For, as we find, these (Mary and Zebedee) were one of the house of Judah and the other of the house or lineage of Levi. Hence the close associations with those of the priesthood. Yet, by and through the associations of Zebedee, there were the contacts with the Essenes and those groups that held rather to a more universality of application of the tenets and teachings of the peoples during the period.

"Hence in such an environment we find that the entity 'entered' during that period just *after* the birth of the Master to Joseph and Mary of the household of Judah. The entity was between James and John—hence during that period when the Master, Jesus, was in Egypt; the place (of birth) being outside of Jerusalem, nigh unto Bethany. Hence we see how that the environs for Naomi in the early portion of its experience in that land were under a *varied* effect. Here we find *something* of the conditions that surrounded the activities of those about the entity:

"Owing to the circumstances of the group to which Zebedee, the father, belonged, this necessitated the choosing of a following or vocation somewhat in keeping with the forefathers, as the *custom* ran. Yet the very location of the home or the dwelling belied—or was at variance to—the general customs, owing to the political situations not only as to the Roman rule but because of the edicts that had become rather contrarywise or at variance with —or at cross-purposes with—Herod's ruling then of the portions of Judea that later became known as the Galilean or the Samaritan or a questioned peoples.

"The activities of Zebedee required that the purposes and aims be rather carried on through or by agents. Or, to put in the parlance of the present, Zebedee was rather in the fishing business as a wholesaler than being in active service himself. As indicated or given, that as He passed by He saw James and John with their father Zebedee *mending* their nets, rather were the brothers of Naomi and the father *supervising* and reasoning with the employees as to their activities. For remember the situations: Mary, the mother, was of the priesthood that was renounced by the cousin, John the Baptist, as known; yet the activities with the Essenes demanded (as would be termed in the present) the keeping secret the meetings of the peoples or the adherents during those cross-purposed edicts of the Roman ruler and Herod. But after the death of Herod the Great, when Herod the Less became in power in the political forces, more consideration was brought or given to those who called their meetings in those various manners. These activities came about, then, when Naomi was nigh unto thirty years of age.

"When did the entity first consider its harkening to an echo of itself? Nigh unto its thirtieth year of age. As to the surroundings, we find that the entity's home life was out of the ordinary, even for that period of experience. For it was pulled, as it were, *between* the teachings or the training of the mother and the activities of the father and the brothers, and yet it had associations in the Roman activities as well as a position in the Jewish faith or Jewish activity. Hence we find this as a description of the body: One educated in the schools of those that were the teachers from Carmel, yet associated with those activities of the people about the temple and those who dedicated themselves to the service that was to bring those activities which, to the world today, find themselves exemplified in many ways. In one area, the entity was one of the sisters of 'orders' known as the Catholic—or the Church—in the present; in the other, she was of the orthodox activities of the 'sisters of mercy' among certain Jewish sects. These, then, may give the conditions of the activity in which the entity, Naomi, in its teen years found itself: pulled between the holy activities of the Essenes and the dedicating of self to the faith of the fathers.

"When there first began those activities among John's teachings, we find the entity then joined rather with those of the Essene group, for John first taught that the women who *chose* might dedicate their lives to a specific service. Hence not only the brothers but those employed by the brothers (Peter, Andrew and Judas—not Iscariot) joined in the activities. These were of the fisherfolk who aided in establishing the teachings in and among the people, that held to both the old and the new environs.

"The body then was fair, with gray eyes and dark hair, but brown in its tinge. In mien the body was gentle, and a good cook, a good housekeeper, a wonderful singer, and given to meditations. Not until *after* those teachings of Master, that made for the establishing more of what would be in the present called the 'home' altars, did the entity wed, being then thirty and four years of age. And it was among the groups in Cana when the wedding feast

173

was held that the associations were made which culminated in the home ties for the entity, making for the reconciliation between Mary and Martha and Lazarus also, and the closer association with Elizabeth, the mother of John. In the entity's home, then, did Elizabeth—of its own kinspeople—dwell, during those portions of its activity among the holy women who had dedicated their lives, their bodies, their purposes, their aims, to those changed teachings between John the forerunner and the Master, Jesus. The entity in those environs, then, made for its development during those experiences in the earth during that period.

"As to the various activities to which the entity was joined during the period, that make for or give experiences in the present activity as to the entity's purpose, we find: There is exhibited much of that which was experienced in those days, of oft being seen and not heard, yet keeping that which was given as an example of the women of the period, 'pondering oft in the heart' that they had seen and heard. In making application of the experience in the present: Hold fast to that thou hast purposed, even then, in thy heart of hearts, in thy soul, that as He gave to thee as direct through the associations with those about the entity in the visits, in the passage of activity: 'Abide in me and I in thee, and ye in me—ask and it shall be given thee.'

"As to the activities also as we have given and intimated through these channels, whether John (the beloved, Naomi's brother) would again join in those activities in the earth, we find: The entity, then, by body, by mind, by position, by soul's development, will be joined nigh unto those experiences with those bodies through which and to which the *entity* John (the brother) may come and be known among men."

On October 6, 1937, Cayce told a nineteen-year-old boy:

"Before that we find that which brings into the present experience an activity that may become as the key to the entity's expression in the present sojourn. For during those periods when the Master walked in the earth, the entity was among the Essenes that made for the predictions—yes, the preparations—for the activities that would

174

bring about His entering into the activities in this period. There we find the entity acted then in the capacity of keeping the records and the temple service where the maids as well as the men were kept; or the entity directed or taught according to the tenets of the law as pertaining to *material* things and the laws or tenets pertaining to the *spiritual* things.

"We find the entity's activities there brought into the experience of many that which his activities influenced and will ever influence in the affairs of man, as man, in the earth: a great revolutionary period. As the entity in the present seeks more and more for the greater knowledge of those things that govern the purposes, that govern the desires, that govern the wishes in the experiences of men from the spiritual angle, more and more will there be the inclinations for the abilities of the entity to become as a leader in its affairs or associations with others. The inclinations from that experience in the present to join with groups of every nature or character may become a part of the entity's experience. Do not let these become then rather sectional or sect activities, but let them rather be for the *common* good of all.

"Then the name was Philo, and he to whom much has been given in those expressions in the activities of individuals arose from the entity's sojourn during that experience."

An eleven-year-old boy was, on April 26, 1938, given this information about his soul:

"Before that we find the entity was in the land of promise, as known, during those periods when the Master walked in the earth. The entity then was among those of the priesthood and closely associated or affiliated with the activities of Zacharias. And the entity was the one who announced, by the blowing of the ram's horn, the various services or activities in the temple where there were the morning and evening periods for the sacrifice, when there were the announcings of those various periods when the offerings might be accepted by the priesthood activity or those who acted in the capacity of the sacrificial priests at the altars.

"Hence the entity knew much of those experiences of John and the activities as connected with same, as also

175

of those activities in the temple when the child Jesus was presented before the priests, as was necessary under the Jewish law. Again we find ritual and those things pertaining to the mental or spiritual conditions and experiences becoming a portion of the entity's whole activities during that sojourn.

"The name then was Xaneres—yes, a Grecian; for the entity was of those activities that were of the pure household of the children of Judah but who had been taking on other names in their activities for the preservations of those activities of the Peternians as well as the Samaritans and those particularly who had accepted the Jewish tenets through the study of those things of that particular sect of same called the Essenes. Hence we find, though the entity held himself in good repute with the rest of the leaders through those periods of service, there were the acquaintances with all of those mysterious influences that were given as a portion of the reasons for the coming of the Wise Men and their teachings, as well as the educational values and activities in the experiences of John and of Jesus to become teachers or leaders in and during that experience."

Life Reading 1602-4, done on September 26, 1939, for a woman of forty-one, demonstrates how one can become somewhat aware subconsciously of experiences of previous sojourns and how, to some extent, one becomes an accumulation of them. Cayce began with:

"In giving a detailed biographical sketch of the experience of the entity as Eunice, it would be well that something be indicated as to the background in which the entity developed, so that there may be a better paralleling or drawing from same in the reasoning of the present, as to how those conditions which arose in the experience of Eunice affected the entity so. We find that in the Galilean land—in which the entity found itself, as it became aware of the tenets and the changes that had come about—there was less of what would be termed the Orthodox Jewry or the adherence to the tenets as had been established with the return of the peoples to the Palestine land from the Persian. Yet, the entity was of those peoples who had united with the remnant left in that land of Zebulon during the period of captivity, thus being a mixture (as

176

understood according to the history of the theological nature or phase) of the Jewry and the Samaritan. However, with those adherents of the land becoming more and more imbued with the ideals and tenets of the Essenes, the entity's family then had embraced that phase. The Essenes were a religious order within Jewry and the adherents and near-adherents of same, see?

"This then was to the entity in its early years a problem because there were the continued reports of happenings that were handed down as a part of the family records (for these were by word of mouth rather than from books) of happenings in the Promised land, of the preserving of a people of 'promise'—though they were in captivity—of returning one portion of the family to the land of promise and of how that portion had been preserved because they had maintained their adherence through the changes which had been wrought.

"Then, with the looking for the Savior, through the tenets of that new order, it became something which to the entity induced the feeling—or the attempt—to make such a combination that, to be sure, through the self must be the lineage that were to see and know and hear of this fulfilling of the promise in the day and age and period of the entity's experience.

"Thus with all such expectancy, there was the betrothal and then the birth of the son, who, to the entity, must be one especially endowed with those privileges that were to mean and to bring such an awakening to the people, an awakening which came to the entity through the very associations with Elizabeth, the mother of John, and the friendships of Mary and Joseph in a portion of *their* experience that was a part of not only the conversation but the wonderments and the study of the entity through those early periods of experience in that particular land. And then there came the edict that robbed *all* the mothers of that particular portion of the land, through that which had been a part of the activities of one in the position to direct the activities and counseling of the Wise Men and their conversation and convocation with the king who made the edict. And then the happening.

"This brought into the experience of the entity a spirit of hurt, of hate for those who had—according to the
177

entity—betrayed that knowledge as pertaining to those who were in those positions of having sons who were in those periods in which there was the expectancy and the desire for their fulfilling a long looked for promise. Into the experience in the present, then, this has brought the little jealousies, the little disputations, that are to be eliminated if there would be the full knowledge of and atonement with the Creative Forces.

"During these periods, as conditions developed, when John and Jesus were receiving their trainings in other lands, the entity kept close in touch with the household of Elizabeth. And through that period when she, too, was affected by the very edicts of the king and when there was the change that brought about the death of the king and through those periods when the Romans robbed Elizabeth of her mate—through the death even at the altar, there began to be changes in the outlook of the entity. The attempt to understand *why* those who were supposed to be endued with powers and activities divine should have such things happen to them brought still greater resentment and wonderment. Then again in the periods when Mary and Elizabeth were so desirous of those activities within their homeland as the changes came about and with the journey from the upper part of Galilee to Capernaum, the entity there entered rather into not wholly the intrigues but rather what might be called in the present more of a social activity, owing to the abilities of the entity's mate to make friendships with those in power.

"With the rebuking of Jesus in the house of worship and the imprisonment of John, the entity—with the expectancy again of motherhood—sought greater counsel with Mary, Martha, and those who were closer to the activities—not only of those who had renounced their relationships with the priests but those who were in the position of keeping alive the order of the Essenes. Then in the latter days of Jesus' sojourn in the material plane, the entity saw her child blessed by Him, among those who were set as the ideal manner in which all individuals were to accept their relationships with others—in that pronouncement, 'Unless ye become as little children, ye shall in no wise enter in.'

"These brought periods of searching of self and the

adherence closer to those tenets which had been a part of the experiences of the entity. Yet, with the knowledge that such a one as Magdala had become a close companion of those of the household, there again was brought to the entity that questioning as to, 'How can such things be?' Such questionings, though, were blotted out in those periods when the entity, with Mary, Josie and the other Mary, learned of those things which had brought the conditions to pass in Jerusalem. And as the entity journeyed there and became aware of the turmoils which surrounded those periods of activities, there was a greater leaning upon those who were of that land. For, remember, of the twelve, seven of them came from the entity's *own* land and own acquaintances.

"As the days passed, the entity was among those who were turning then more and more to the tenets pertaining to the activities in Jerusalem. And the Pentecost came. Then the entity was among those who heard her own kinsmen speak in tongues, seeing the great tumult and the activities wrought. Thus there was builded that determination within the experience and heart of the entity to bring the greater knowledge, the greater awareness, of the spirit of truth, as was indeed manifested by Him that shed through the tenets of His disciples and Apostles the new light to men, so that hate and those things that make afraid may be put away, and so that positions of power or wealth or fame may be set as naught compared to the peace that came and *is* the understanding of those who have seen and known and become aware of His presence abiding, even as the entity heard promised, 'Lo, I am with you always, even unto the end of the world.'

"Through the latter portion of its experience, then, we find that the entity ministered to the needs of the saints, as they were called, or those who dedicated their lives and their activities wholly to the ministering to the fields about the whole of that land. The entity thus gained in the giving—giving of self, in just being kind to those who were heavily burdened by the cares of life, whether in illness or in the vicissitudes of relationships or in wants of the body or in needs in the activities of others that brought desperate circumstance in the experience.

"These, then, should be analyzed, and the petty jeal-

179

ousies and hates made less and less a part of the attitudes of mind and body and activities in the present. Meeting all of those forces in the experiences, we find that the entity —Eunice—was among the elderly mothers of the church in the latter portion of the experience, in the southern-most portion of Palestine. Thus we find that the associations with those who were in authority of the Romans and those who were brought to a better understanding by the associations of the wife of Cornelius, who brought the great activity and blessings to many of the entity's house-hold and friends—all these brought in the experience of the entity the joys in which it passed into the greater realms of activity in that experience."

Cayce then said he was ready for questions. The woman wanted to know whether, in the present sojourn, her soul-mind would derive the greatest spiritual benefits through relationships with other entities who had been associated with Jesus or John or those in authority during the Palestinian experience. Cayce told her:

"All of these must be met by circumstances. These may be found, as individuals, by paralleling the lives and experiences of those who were in that particular period—not that these are to be chosen as individuals but they are the activities that are a part of the experience. To be sure, there is what may be called an excess of that urge arising from such activities, but as to whether it shall be applied in the direct associations of individuals or as a cause or purpose, in contact with those things and influences that bring a united effort, is to be the choice of the entity itself.

"For, this: Because of the associations with those in authority back then, as counselors, we find that in the presence of such individuals in the *present* there is felt the urge, 'Well, I can't get that, nor those activities.' But those are principles and not things to be applied as to individuals. If there are things to be worked *out*, with individuals, because of the knowledge of same, then as to whether or not this is attempted depends upon the choice in self, as to whether such knowledge is to be a stumbling-block or a steppingstone for greater development. Test not self beyond what it is able to bear. Rather develop for the *principle* than for the activity of individuals.

180

"In analyzing the present experience and environ, it will be seen that the associations are with some to whom the entity ministered much and brought through such activity greater blessings to many. Thus, where such are needed, apply thyself. When there is the urge because of the personalities of individuals that renew the urge for activities known within self to be such as to cause or make one to err, remember as He gave, 'Being forewarned, be forearmed, and allow not thine house (thine *self*) to be broken up.' "

The woman said: "I have had visions and impressions of a Roman experience during the period immediately following that of the Palestine. Is this so or is it the same?"

Cayce said: "As we find, it is rather the visioning of the experience the entity had with those who were in authority. Remember, as was first given, in the early portion of the experience the entity heard both sides that were handed down—as the experience of those in the Chaldean land as well as those in the land of promise. In the latter portion the entity heard from those in authority (as Cornelius and those of his household) about the activities in Rome and how such were carried on. Hence it is as a vision by the entity rather than an experience of being in the position. For, as we find, if analyzed, the vision is rather the awareness of such a position, yet not being in Rome itself."

In 1934, Cayce was doing a check Reading for Mrs. 2072, then thirty-four, and, referring to both herself and her husband, she asked: "What were our names in the Palestine period?"

Cayce said: "Ruth and what should be called in the present Alec, for he was a pretty smart aleck then." He almost smiled.

"Were we Essenes in the Palestine period?"

"The names themselves imply it, yes. But remember the Essenes had the divisions, just as you will find that most churches have their groups and divisions. These two were in opposite groups of the Essenes. One held that a thing can happen; the other held that God makes it happen. Which comes first, the hen or the egg? As was implied in that same question."

181

"What were our activities as Essenes?"

"As is indicated, they were so divided that comparing them together isn't well. And as to using in the present, don't fall out with each other because one wants to listen to Brahms and the other to Liszt." Many times Cayce resorted to this kind of homespun wisdom in the effort to make people distinguish between important and unimportant differences, even in matters of religion, thereby making him an ecumenist ahead of his time.

On October 17, 1942, a follow-up was done on the Life Reading of Mrs. 2175, thirty-one, and it had already been established that she had been the nurse of John the Baptist. She now wanted more information about that. So Cayce told her:

"In giving the outline and the activities of the entity through the experience in Palestine, something of the history of the period must be interpreted, for this to be a helpful experience for the entity.

"There were, in the period, those political turmoils with many of those peoples of the holy family—or the house of the Lord. Zachariah was a just man, then living in the hills of Galilee, and he was the priest who offered sacrifice for the month of Nisan. And when there were those visions or experiences and his wife Elizabeth conceived, these brought into the experience of those groups —of which this entity, Sofa, was a part, the Essenes— a great deal of questioning, as to what manner of individual would be required or needed as the helper or director or nurse, in the circumstances that would naturally arise if these visions were to be fulfilled.

"When there had been the experience, then, of the happening of the visit of Mary to Elizabeth, there was the choosing of the dedicated women for this office. This was a reminder to many of what and how the maiden had been chosen on the stair. The entity then, Sofa, was one of the women dedicated to service in the temple, not as one that would be called a caretaker but these were the offices of the entity—to 'touch up' or paint or to keep certain portions of the temple in order for the activities of the priest. Thus the entity appealed to Zachariah to use his period of preparation as the one to offer the sacrifice, as the time when there would be the choosing of the

182

attendant or nurse to the babe. Hence the entity was chosen by what would be termed—or is termed in the Cabala—the moving of the symbols upon the vesture of the priest. This, then, prevented *any* of those confusions as might have arisen with the entity.

"When there was the birth, then, of John (for, remember, he was not called the Baptist until after his death), in the periods of training the entity also acted as the instructor, as in the position of one who looks after or cares for those through such periods. And (this aside) too often there is not sufficient thought taken as to the care of a developing body through those first eighteen months to two years. Here, though, this entity was chosen by those directing forces as from the temple service itself —or by divine guidance. Thus did the entity fulfill, until the boy, John, was weaned at six years of age.

"Then the entity was associated with Jesus with the last year of the experience in the household of Mary and Joseph. While the offices here had been fulfilled by that one as we have indicated, the entity was especially given this office to indicate to the developing child the nature, the character, of the cousin. After that period and the period of education and the periods when the labor began, from the periods of twelve years to that of seventeen, when the entity John went to Egypt for the dedication and the preparation there, the entity was known among those who were as holy women, who acted in the capacity of the mourners at the various functions of the Order, as would be called, of the Essenes.

"Later the entity was among those—not *the* first but *among* the first—to be baptized by John in Jordan. The entity also ministered to the needs of John when he was cast in prison and was among the chief mourners when he was beheaded. The entity also was among those who, during His period in prison, sought Jesus for counsel. And with the answers given, the entity was confused, until there were those reclaiming activities upon the day of Pentecost. Then the entity was old in years and among those first disturbed by the first edicts that brought death to James. The entity died in that period from exposure by the abuse of soldiers in that first raid.

"As to the period, no losses in spiritual or mental progress might be indicated; rather those periods of confusion could be the experience of any that are dedicated to an idea and who in sincerity give of their best through a material sojourn. As so the entity's parents, these were of the Levites and those acquainted with many of the activities in the temple. And from same, ceremony means much to the entity. Whatever the preparation, for whatever the function, to the entity there must be some ceremony. Ready for qustions."

The woman asked: "To what extent and over what period of time did I have a close association with Jesus?"

"As indicated, during a year the entity gave most of the time to indicating to the child Jesus the life, the preparation and the character of John, and then *only* meeting same in those periods when, as indicated, coming to Him for counsel."

"In choosing to be the nurse of John the Baptist—"

Cayce interrupted her. "Chosen. Not choosing but *asking* that there *be* a choosing, and chosen by the office —or upon the ephod."

"Did I take the vows of celibacy?"

"They didn't take the vows of celibacy! Not to have children during those periods was considered to be ones not thought of by God."

_ "Concerning the fulfillment of those promises which had been a part of the Scripture, please outline the promises for purposes of study. That is, where in the Bible?"

"*All* of those recorded by the writers respecting the visit of the disciples of John to Jesus; then especially fourteenth, fifteenth, sixteenth and seventeenth of John. *There* are the promises that are a part of the promises to the entity. And to all."

A forty-two-year-old woman who consulted Edgar Cayce for the first time on August 25, 1943, found that she, too, had occupied a unique role in the life of Jesus. Cayce told her:

"Before that the entity was in the Holy Land during those days when the Master walked in the earth and was among those people when there was the choosing of the disciples. The entity was acquainted with the Master, being a sister of Peter's wife's mother. Thus the entity was acquainted with the first of the outward miracles of

184

healing in that experience and has looked for——and may find——in its own hands the abilities to heal others in His name. Not of self but in His name.

"In the experience the entity ever remained through the period one of those of the holy women. The timidity, the backwardness, and yet the exaltation, which may be the experience of many by merely being in the presence of the entity, arises from that sojourn. For, as has been indicated, all feel a variation, a difference, by the very presence of the entity in any company. This is not to be used other than as given: kindness, gentleness, patience, persistence and brotherly love. These are the fruits of the spirit. These ye then made manifest. These ye may again make manifest.

"There, too, the entity made for much color, and it was this entity that prepared the robe of the piece for the Master. The name then was Martha."

A year later, on June 17, 1944, "Martha" (3175) was the subject of a third reading, and Cayce gave this information:

"In giving the experiences of the entity in the earth plane as Martha, the sister of Peter's wife's mother, it would be well that much of the happenings or history of the times be included, so that there may be the more perfect understanding of the conditions and as to how and why urges from that experience apply in the experience of the entity in the present. As is understood by many, there had been long a looking forward to or for the advent of the promised Messiah into the earth and there had been those various groups through one channel or another who had banded together to study the material which was handed down through the varied groups in that day and period.

"Here we find there had been, for the mother of Martha, an experience of coming in touch with Judy, who had been the first of women appointed as the head of the Essenes group to have the experience of having 'voices,' which would be called in the present experiences 'communications' with the influences which had been a part of man's experience from the beginning, such as that the divine *within* man heard the experiences of those forces *outside* of man and communicated in voices, in

185

dreams, in signs and symbols which had become a portion of the experience.

"When the children of Martha's mother, Sophia, were in those periods of development these (communications) had become a part of what would be called today a 'play-experience' for the entity Martha. For Peter's wife's mother was many years the senior of Martha, but the coming of John and the birth of Jesus and the dispensation of Jesus and John in Egypt all had an impression or imprint upon the mind of the entity Martha, who builded in her own mind how the king and how the announcer of the king should be dressed (as this had been a part of the experiences of the entity in other periods and thus the choice of things in this direction).

"Then there came those great changes in the life experience of Martha, for one among those of the rulers of the synagogue sought the entity in marriage and through the individuals who made these arrangements the entity was espoused to Nicodemus. Through his activities and personality, Martha learned first of what had happened to the peoples in the homes of John the Baptist and of Mary and Joseph and Jesus. Then when there were later the experiences of those entering into activities and then when the message was given out that Martha's older sister had been healed from a terrible fever by this man Jesus, this brought about great changes in Nicodemus and Martha, as they had to do with the temple and the service of the high priest. Martha began the weaving of the robe that became as a part of the equipment the Master had. Thus the robe was made especially for the Master. In color it was not as the robe of the priest, but woven in the one piece with the hole in the top through which the head was to be placed, and then over the body so that with the cords it was bound about the waist.

"This robe Nicodemus presented then to the Master, Jesus, after the healing of the widow of Nain's son, who was a relative of Nicodemus. In the activities, then, when Nicodemus went to the Master by night and there became those discussions in the home, for Nicodemus and Martha there began the communion as man and wife rather than man and his chattel of his servant. They were more on a basis of equality, not in the same proportions

186

which were established a bit later by some of the rulers from the Roman land but more in keeping with the happenings which had brought about the activities in the Essene group.

"Though Martha was an Essene, Nicodemus never accepted completely the tenets or the teachings of the Essenes group. These were a part of the principles and applications of Martha. The acquaintanceships, the friendships, which were established between Mary, Elizabeth and the other Mary all are parts of the experience, and because of the position of Martha throughout those activities she was considered rather one of the leaders—or one to whom others made appeal to have positions or conditions set in motion so that there was given more concessions to the Holy Women who followed Jesus from place to place when there were those periods of His Palestine ministry.

"The only differences which arose were with Martha and Mary in the household of Lazarus, Martha and Mary. Because of conditions there from which Mary (Magdalene) had returned, from the houses which were a portion of her activity in various cities, questions as to morality arose. And yet, after there were the healings and after it was discovered how she out of whom seven devils were cast became changed and how there were even changes then and there, we find there was a greater working together with the activities of Mary, Martha, Lazarus and Mary the mother of Jesus, Elijah and many of those others, including John and Mark's mother. These were parts of the experience of the entity.

"The entity stood, as indicated by the accomplishments of the robe from Nicodemus, as one particularly honored even by the Master. During the periods of activity, during the missions after the Crucifixion and Resurrection of the Master, the entity Martha gathered with those in the upper room looking for the promise of the coming of the outpouring of the Holy Spirit. This, too, became a part of the activities. For the entity later was among those who aided Stephen and Philip, as well as others of the various lands. For it was with these that the entity first became acquainted with Luke and Lucius, who later became heads of various organizations in other portions.

187

These acquaintances were then rather as counsel from those to whom Luke, Lucius, Mark as the younger of the Disciples (not Apostles but younger of the Disciples) went for counsel. For the entity was one acquainted with the law. The entity Martha taught the law to the young ones, the children who sought knowledge.

"The entity had its own family—two sons and one daughter. These became ministers in the church in Antioch, aiding the peoples who worked with Barnabas; and it is mentioned that one, Theopolus, learned from the entity Sylvanus; and those who labored in the church in Jerusalem with John, James, Peter and the others, as a child. As a child, this one was known as Thaddeus. The daughter was wed to one of the companions of Paul, Silas, who was engaged in a portion of the activities with Paul.

"As to the activities of the entity, then: The abilities are indicated in weaving, in color. The color of the robe was pearl-gray, as would be called now, with selvage woven around the neck, as well as that upon the edge, as over the shoulder and to the bottom portion of same; no bells, no pomegranates, but those which are woven in such a manner that into the selvage portion of the bottom were woven the Thummin and the Urim. These were as the balance in which judgments were passed by the priest. But these were woven, not placed, upon the top of same. Neither were there jewels set in same.

"With the persecution, the entity withdrew more and more because of its associations with those in authority, but its home became more and more a place of refuge and help for all of the young of the church. The entity lived to be an elderly person, something like seventy-nine years of age in the experience, and was not among those ever beaten or placed in jail, though persecuted by only the Romans, feared by those of her own peoples. Ready for questions."

The woman asked: "Are any of the children of that period associated with the entity in the present?"

"These will become associated with the entity, not in the present."

"What place did I occupy at the Crucifixion?"

"As one of those upon the right hand of Mary, the

Mother of Jesus, and the other Mary upon the left hand."

"In the meeting on the day of Pentecost?"

"Among those who heard all of the various places announce their hearing Peter in their own tongue."

"In what way was I acquainted with Lucius?"

"As indicated, as a teacher, as a helper, an advisor, when he was destined by being joined in the church activities in his own home areas. The entity never visited there."

"Any other advice?"

"Keep close to those things which draw thee nearer to the Cross of Christ. For it is in Him, through Him, ye each have thy being. As He accepted the work of thine hands then, may He accept the work of thy hands in the present."

On March 29, 1944, a second Reading was done for No. 3344, a man then forty-six, and it contains a reference to certain circumstances which may now be of tremendous significance in terms of the Qumran literature. The copper scrolls have been identified by scholars as a list of a hidden treasure, a treasure so vast that it probably could not have belonged to the Essenes. It should be pointed out, however, that the Essenes lived the communal life and anyone joining the sect was expected to turn over his possessions for use by the community. Since the first Christians also lived the community life, this same gesture was undoubtedly expected of them. In view of the likelihood that Pentecost was followed by a great surge of conversions, a passage in the following Reading, which is underscored, can throw new light on the mysterious copper scrolls.

Cayce said:

"We find that the entity Philas was of that group of people from Seleucia who came to Jerusalem during those days of the Pentecost when there was an outpouring of the Holy Spirit upon the Apostles who had been warned to tarry in Jerusalem until that day. The entity was among those who were students of the law, those who were interested in the activities having to do with questionings pertaining to the law that had been interpreted from the priests and rabbis of the day, pertaining to the Mosiac law, and the interesting facts and fancies that had

189

come from the eastern lands, from which the Wise Men had come. These, as parts of the teachings, had become adopted by those groups of Essenes of which John and Joseph and Mary had been a part before the entering of the Master, Jesus, in the earth.

"With Stephen, Philip and others, the entity was among those chosen of the young men; Philas at the time being only a little past nineteen years of age. Thus we find the entity was not acquainted directly with the individuals until this period who had been associated with the Master as Disciples, now Apostles, or those who had been very close to the activity. As a student, though, the entity was aroused to the possibilities and probabilities of the activities to which the individuals might give themselves or contribute to—or gain something from—as to add to the interest in living.

"Philas was of a group not wholly Jewish or Grecian but one interested in same because of the background genealogically of the things happening. The entity journeyed to Jerusalem because of the interest aroused by hearsay and the expectancy among the peoples, the great throngs. On the journey, the entity became closely identified or associated with Stephen, who, after the joining of so many to the efforts of the Disciples or Apostles on the day of Pentecost, *became the treasurer of the organization that became a necessity, in that record keepers had to be appointed because of the great amount of contributions of various natures to those people.* Stephen and Philip and Philas and others had been chosen by the Disciples or Apostles to attend to the needs of the great throngs of people.

"There were those chosen who were entirely of the circumcision. There were those chosen who were of the uncircumcised group, yet were identified with services in various forms, in that which had been adopted by the Samaritan Jews as well as Grecian Jews, who were only part Jews. Some of these facts became the problems (that were unnecessary in their particular activity or for their beliefs) in the teachings of Peter, John and James, who were the chief spokesmen during those periods following the outpouring of the Holy Spirit on the day of Pentecost.

"With these activities there came for the entity questions from some of the Apostles, in that the entity, Philas, used the position to which he had been appointed as a means for social relationships with the various groups of women, the girls, that were a part of the activities through those particular periods. These brought questionings. They also brought into the experience of the entity some of those very conditions that are a part of the entity's present experience—as to the sincerity of purposes in the oaths taken and the living up to same because of seeming negligence on the part of either or both concerning in the martial relationships. Hence the entity is meeting its own self in the present.

"In some groups there was not just the one factor but rather a questioning as there had been among many of those in the early church, in portions of the land from which the entity came, as in Loadicea, Thyatira, as in all of those where there were the mixed relationships of Greeks, Romans, Jews, Sirophoenicians or the followers of the eastern tenets of those peoples, as to their relationship with the opposite sex.

"These, then, are the problems to be met. These were the problems causing the questionings, rather than the honesty or sincerity in which the entity as Philas administered the contributions. The greater disturbance arose after the martyrdom of Stephen. This drew the entity closer and closer to the needs of the people, but because of the persecution many of the groups were scattered throughout the various lands and the entity returned to its own land, becoming engaged in those activities that brought about a great contribution, for the entity was engaged in the tilling of the soil and the usage of teachings or tenets of both the old and new dispensations, as well as the legends of the East."

Finally, there was a Reading done on June 28, 1932, in the Cayce home on Arctic Crescent in Virginia Beach, and present at it were numerous members of Norfolk Study Group No. 1 of the Association for Research and Enlightenment. The purpose of the Reading was mostly to give the members a demonstration of the phenomenon, and, to add to the interest, the subject chosen was of special interest to them all. Nobody in the room realized

191

that during the Reading something would be said that would become fact in another fifteen years, something whose full value has even now still to be determined.

After Cayce had gone into trance, Gertrude Cayce began in the usual way: "You will please give at this time an outline of the life and activities of Jesus the Christ from the time of His birth until the beginning of His ministry in Palestine at approximately thirty years of age, giving birth place, training, travels, and so on."

Cayce said: "As seen from the records that were kept then regarding the promises and their fulfillments in many lands, 'Thou Bethlehem of Judah—the birth place of the Great Initiate, the Holy One, the Son of man, the Accepted One of the Father.' During those periods in accordance with those laws and rulings, in the household of the father. Then in the care and the ministry from the period of the visit to Jerusalem, in first India, then Persia, then Egypt, for 'My son shall be called from Egypt.' Then a portion of the sojourn with the forerunner that was first proclaimed in the region about Jordan; and then the return to Capernaum, the city of the beginning of the ministry. Then in Canaan and Galilee. In the studies that were a portion of the preparation, these included first those that were the foundations of that given as law. Hence from law in the Great Initiate must come love, mercy, peace, that there may be the fulfilling wholly of that purpose to which, of which, He was called."

"From what period and how long did He remain in India?"

"From thirteen to sixteen. One year in travel and in Persia; the greater portion being in the Egyptian. In this, the greater part will be seen in the records that are set in the pyramids there, for *here* were the initiates taught."

"Under whom did He study in India?"

"Kshjiar."

"Under whom in Persia?"

"Junner."

"In Egypt?"

"Zar."

"Outline the teachings which were received in India."

"Those cleansings of the body as related to preparation for strength in the physical as well as in the mental man. In the travels and in Persia, the unison of forces as related to those teachings of that given in those of Zu and Ra. In Egypt, that which had been the basis of all the teachings in those of the temple, and the after actions of the crucifying of self in relationships to ideals that made for the abilities of carrying on that called to be done. In considering the life physical of any of the teachers, these should not be looked upon by students as unnatural conditions; rather as the righteous Father *calling* to those that had builded in their experience that enabling them to become what all individuals *must* in their own little sphere, gradually enlarging same to become inclusive until they —the individuals—are one in purpose, one in aim, one in ideal, with Him."

"In which pyramid are the records of the Christ?"

"That yet to be uncovered."

"What relation was there in the training with the three Wise Men?"

"Representing the three phases of the development, for these were those that looked toward that development, as is symbolized by the character of that given as the blessings were made upon the infant in the manger."

"Are there any written records which have not been found of the teachings?"

"More, rather, of those of the close associates, and those records that are yet to be found of the preparation of the man, of the Christ, in those of the tomb or those yet to be uncovered in the pyramid."

"When will this chance be given for these to be uncovered?"

"When there has been sufficient of the 'reckoning' through which the world is passing in the present. Thirtysix . . . thirty-eight . . . forty. . . ." He was less than ten years off.

"He said He would come again. What about His second coming?"

"The time no one knows. Even as He gave, not even the Son Himself. *Only* the Father. Not until His enemies —and the earth—are wholly in subjection to His will, His powers."

"Are we entering the period of preparation for His coming?"

"Entering the test period, rather."

"Any message to the group gathered here?"

"In that ye seek to know the manner of preparation of Him that would be your guide, seek also to prepare *yourselves* to be His subjects with that same diligence as that which has prompted the seeking here. We are through."

Gladys Davis took the shorthand notes of this Reading, as she had done thousands of times before and was to do thousands of times again. As usual, she waited until Edgar Cayce awoke, and then she read him her notes, for his own information as well as his approval. After the meeting disbanded, she went to her office and typed the transcript and showed it to Cayce, again for his approval. He told her something. She went back to her desk and added this to the transcript:

"GD's memo: While I read aloud my notes to those present, EC saw a vision of white figure, size of a man, coming from ocean; he went right through cars and all objects—came down the street past Pacific toward us and disappeared just as I stopped reading."

TEN

Contradictions arise.

Pliny says that Essenes did not engage in business and would "not even dream of carrying on traffic, innkeeping or navigation, for they repudiate every inducement of covetousness." But the Edgar Cayce Readings show that the innkeeper at Bethlehem was an Essene. The Qumran literature pertains only to the monastic life of Essenes, creating the impression for some scholars that all Essenes were cloistered. But Josephus said that four thousand Essenes lived throughout the country. There was, for that matter, a "Gate of Essenes" in the walled city of Jerusalem. All firsthand commentators on the Essenes write about the communal aspect of the sect: All things were owned in common—there were no rich and no poor. Yet Zebedee was a rich man, a businessman. The Readings indicate that this may have been a "front"—allowing a prominent businessman to maintain contact with orthodoxy in order to keep up with any developments in high places which might affect the Essenes. An Essene had been planted in Herod's palace for the same reason. Moreover, all Essenes had to work at something. Zebedee could have hired a manager to run the business; but he was there working with his men when Jesus first approached. Even Mary, who certainly must have been revered by all Essenes, worked in the library while in Egypt and helped with the serving of the wedding feast at Cana. And Jesus, who was accepted as the Messiah by the Essenes even before He was born, was nevertheless known at the beginning of His ministry as the carpenter from Nazareth. Ordinarily this would have kept Him at the bottom of the social ladder, but soon His rich friends were criticizing him for associating so much with the poor.

So contradictions arise. Sometimes, however, the contradictions arise not so much from the evidence as from the personal attitudes of the people who are appraising the evidence. This is inescapable. Despite the great contributions to history made by the Qumran literature, there are still too many gaps in history and in the literature itself for the experts to put aside their debate and reach an agreement on what happened back in those days and how the events back in those days pertained to the life of Jesus. Until the gaps are filled, objectivity can hardly be expected even from men of science who nevertheless hold to certain religious convictions.

The scholar who probably has been most vocal on this point is Professor John Allegro, of the University of Manchester, England, a man who has done considerable work on the Qumran literature. Acknowledging himself to be a man of no religious denominational affiliation, Professor Allegro has often charged that Christian churches, as organizations, have been remiss in supporting the Qumran research, perhaps out of the apprehension that the ultimate facts might shake the foundations of Christianity today. Though there may be some basis for the accusation, at least in terms of providing funds, it must be conceded, on the other hand, that much of the Dead Sea research has been done by scientists, some of them clergymen, from church-associated universities, and who for years have been freed from class work in order to concentrate their efforts and skills in the field, and this may be a contribution to the project. Moreover, the area has not been entirely peaceful over the past twenty years and a full-scale scientific assault has not been feasible, even had the money been available. It would seem, however, that if the Qumran literature has thus far produced any evidence which might shake up Christianity there would be some difficulty in keeping it secret. And what is there to be shaken?

In its article on Essenes, the Catholic Encyclopedia comments: "There have been many unsubstantiated hypotheses about their (the Essenes') influence on Christianity. The Dead Sea Scrolls, however, show grounds for suspecting considerable indirect influence, which does nothing to destroy the originality of Christianity." Some experts hold that the Dead Sea Scrolls actually support the originality of Christianity to a considerable extent, whether "originality" is defined as beginnings or uniqueness. A great deal of supportive evidence existed before the discovery of the Qumran literature, which can become clear by making comparisons between the Bible and the comments of those who wrote about the Essenes in their own time.

For example, both the Essenes and the first Christians held similar attitudes toward communal living, the sacramental aspect of bathing or baptism, in prophecy, in preexistence or reincarnation, in resurrection and immortality, in the casting out of devils, spiritual healing, the working of miracles, the power of prayer, in the equality of mankind, and in a kind of predestination in that all things happen in the fullness of time and can be foreseen.

The Essenes and the first Christians used the same greetings: "Peace be with you." Several times in the Gospels, Jesus is quoted as saying this; He said it again

196

when appearing to the Apostles in the upper room after His resurrection. The Essenes were opposed to taking oaths; Herod the Great excused them from an oath of allegiance to him, knowing he could take them at their word. In Matthew 5, Jesus says: "You are not to swear at all. . . . Plain 'Yes' or 'No' is all you need to say. Anything beyond that comes from the devil."

Just as the Essenes eschewed wealth, Jesus told a rich young man to sell all he had, give the money to the poor, then follow Him. Jesus said it would be easier for a camel to enter the eye of a needle than for a rich man to enter the kingdom of God. Just as the Essenes had their brotherly meal of bread and must, Jesus and the Apostles had their 'Last Supper,' and the early Christians called their similar meal the "agape"—the feast of love.

The list is endless.

Professor Millar Burrows, the Winkley Professor of Biblical Theology, at Yale University, and a recognized expert on the Dead Sea Scrolls, once remarked that after seven years of intensive study of the Scrolls and fragments he had not come upon any information which, in his opinion, would require any changes in basic Christian tenets. He said:

"The history of our religion is no less a history of God's work if it is shown to be a continuous process involving contacts, relationships and development. As a matter of fact, Christian theologians have never thought of it as anything other than that. They have always been more or less aware, and increasingly so of late, that Christianity is closely related to other religions at many points and has acquired and assimilated much from other religions. It arose in the first place within Judaism and was first offered to Jews by Jews as the true Judaism, not as replacing but as fulfilling the faith of their fathers. Jesus was the one for whom Moses and the prophets looked."

But, as Burrows points out, the theologians know this, but the average layman doesn't. So the layman becomes alarmed when he hears informed and reputable men like Allegro, like Edmund Wilson, like Bible Scholar A. Powell-Davis, suggest that, because of the Dead Sea Scrolls, it is now apparent that many of the basic Chris-

197

epts were not original with Jesus and that thus
not have been who He said He was and that there-
ristianity has had a shaky foundation all along.

rows intimates that some of the Qumran literature
is being withheld, but he does not say why. It has been
acknowledged that not all of the information uncovered
during the excavations of the three towns on the plain
beyond Qumran has been disclosed, but again it is not
known why. Since almost all of the Qumran findings are
now in Israeli hands, any Christian sensitivities about the
data become irrelevant, and this applies as well to any
information the Arabs may have. The likelihood of keeping secret for long any Qumran evidence regarding the
divinity of Jesus, one way or the other, is indeed remote;
but the lingering secrecy in Jerusalem does create the
eerie suspicion that perhaps the Scriptures have been
tampered with.

They have. As Burrows puts it, anybody who believes
that the King James Version of the Bible is infallible
simply doesn't know the facts. This applies as well to
Douay and to the ancient Greek and Hebrew texts on
which present translations are based. This is something
else theologians have known for a long time; the Qumran
writings confirmed it. Though the editing appears to be
minor, there still has been some editing, and there might
have been much more than now appears. Perhaps this is
the secret in Jerusalem.

There has been another kind of tampering. The Qumran writings establish that the Essenes treasured the Book
of Enoch. The Acts of the Apostles show that the first
Christians also treasured it. In the Third Christian Century, the Fathers and Apologists of the Church decided
that the book was not canonical and it was dropped
from the Bible. Copies of it disappeared, and it was not
seen again until a British explorer found an Ethiopian
version of it in that country in 1773. The book is distinctly Essenic because it is so specifically Messianic. It
appears to have been written by four different authors
over a period of almost two hundred years, which was
one of the reasons it was not adjudged canonical.

In terms of the Essenic-Christian relationship, the Book
of Enoch is important both for history and for content.

Exegetes agree that the first sections were written in the last third of the Second Century B. C. by a pious Jew who lived in the Land of Dan near the headwaters of the Jordan in the general area that became Galilee. His opinions make him sound Hasidim, one of the pious Jews who fled north from Juda to get away from the corruption and persecution. These people were the precursors of the Pharisees. Later portions are definitely Pharisaic regarding the type of Messiah who would come; but then the writing becomes almost Sadducean, omitting references to a Messiah. The last part, written between 95 B. C. and 65 B. C., resumes the Pharisaic expectation of a Messiah, discusses Enoch's visions, and complains about the slaying of the "righteous." When the book is read with the Essenes in mind, it falls into place historically; out of the Essenic context, it has a tone of doubtful validity. Valid or not, the Early Fathers, by banning the book, erased from history a large slice of knowledge that would have provided an important link in the Essenic progression to Christianity.

Also banned was a companion writing, the Book of the Secrets of Enoch, of which no copies were known for almost fifteen hundred years, until five manuscripts were found in Russia and Servia. This book is even more Essenic. It tells of Enoch's visit to the seven heavens and how God told him about the creation of the world, about the fallen angels, and gives him the rudiments of cosmology and astrology. Returning to earth, Enoch gives this information to his sons and, among other things, tells them not to take oaths. Assuring them of the coming of the Messiah, Enoch returns to heaven, and there is rejoicing among his people. The book was probably written in Egypt between 30 B. C. and A. D. 70.

When one considers how strangely these two books disappeared from circulation, one considers that it is equally strange that the four authors of the Gospels, who go to such lengths to prove the divinity of Jesus, give no attention to the years of His life between twelve and thirty. Was this intentional? Was it an oversight? Was it editing?

There has always been a portion of the sacred literature which has been withheld from the general public.

In the time of Jesus, the hidden literature was known as the cabal or cabala and was oral tradition supposedly handed down from Abraham. It is known that Paul studied the cabal under Gamaliel, then president of the Sanhedrin and an advocate of leniency toward Christians. This cabal, it is said, contained some Christian references, such as the concept of a Divine Trinity. Later, when the Early Fathers were putting the Bible together around the start of the Fourth Christian Century, it is known that they agreed among themselves not to discuss in public some of the books they had read and banned because some of them were so mystical, so heady, that they could endanger the soul of the average person who could not understand them and might be led astray. Teilhard de Chardin was banned for the same reason. Perhaps there has been too much caution, with the result that Christianity has been simplified to a point of Christmas-card sweetness which can be enjoyed comfortably among friends without the burden of corrective efforts in a world torn by war, hate, violence, extremism and injustice in every land.

Most Qumran experts agree that John the Baptist was an Essene. But if the Essenes were a monastic order, what was John doing at the Jordan? Did he leave the order? Was he dismissed? Was there about to be another division within the Essenes, as there had been numerous times over preceding centuries?

Opinions among the experts on the relationship of Jesus and the Essenes vary, usually reflecting the individual expert's personal religious convictions. Some—the "radicals," perhaps—say that Jesus was indeed an Essene, that He had grown up in a monastery, probably at Qumran, and that, around thirty, He either decided that He was the Messiah or was persuaded of it or merely became aware of it, and then went out to begin His ministry, His cousin John accompanying Him. Those holding varieties of this opinion feel that Jesus was certainly a holy man, a good man, a wise man, but He was not of the Divine and that the church He started was eventually influenced far more by the Apostle Paul than by Himself. Others—the "conservatives"—say that Jesus obviously was familiar with Essenic life and thought; but that certainly He, Mary and Joseph knew even before He was born that He was of the Divine, He was the Messiah, and that, as such, He would not have joined any Jewish sect but would have waited quietly at Nazareth until the fullness of His time had come to begin—to originate—what is now called Christianity. Perhaps the truth is a combination of both ideas. For many Christians, the sensitive areas would be the Divinity of Jesus and the originality of His church.

Edgar Cayce was extremely aware of these sensitivities, even in trance. In trance, he told a writer not to call her biography of Jesus "Jesus The Essene" because this would be offensive to a lot of people. Out of offense, people might refuse to give serious consideration to the possibility of an experience which in no way would have detracted from the uniqueness of Jesus as the Son of God, the Son of Man, the Savior. Cayce was equally aware of the sensitivities of many Christians on the lifelong virginity of Mary, realizing that, again out of offense, some people would refuse to give serious consideration to the possibility that the experience of subsequently having other children by Joseph in no way detracted from her uniqueness as the Chosen Vessel of the Messiah by means of a valid virgin birth.

An impressive factor about the Edgar Cayce Readings is that so many of the details have subsequently been confirmed by the Qumran literature. For example, before the discovery of the Dead Sea Scrolls, no acknowledged expert in history or religion ever put forth the possibility that Jesus, Mary, Joseph, John the Baptist and other leading figures in the Gospels were associated in any way with the Essenes. The Edgar Cayce Readings, however, had been producing information regarding the association for over twenty years. Soon after the content of the scrolls became known, numerous experts, Burrows and Allegro among them, were quick to recognize the similarities between the Qumran writings and the New Testament. It became unquestionable that John the Baptist had been an Essene, and some suggest that he might have left the monastery after some disagreement. The influence of the Essenes upon Jesus also became clear, and again some experts suggest that He, too, might have broken with the sect over some difference in views. According to the Cayce Readings, though all Essenes were not of one viewpoint, there would be nothing unusual in having two Essenes living and working outside a monastery: Jesus and John were simply carrying out their individual roles in the Divine Plan.

The consensus today that Jesus and John were at least greatly influenced by the Essenes produces further food for thought. The extent of the influence, as evidenced in comparing the Qumran writings and the New Testament, could only have resulted from intimate contact. The Bible tells nothing about John between the occasion of his prenatal presence, when Mary visited Elizabeth, and the occasion when we meet him at the Jordan. The life of Jesus between the ages of twelve and thirty is not described in the Bible. If, then, Jesus and John spent their youth as students with the Essenes, they could only have done so with the consent and the desire of their parents, since the community's rules required that children be submitted by their parents at an early age. This indicates that Mary and Joseph and Elizabeth and Zachary would at least have been sympathetic toward the Essenes if not actual members of the sect, which the Readings say they were. That the four authors of the Gospels were either Essenes or profoundly Essene influenced is also the consensus now.

Another area of confirmation is particularly specific. It is the area of astrology. In numerous Readings, Cayce said that the Essenes, including Jesus, studied astrology. In 1938, during a Reading for the entity who had been Josie, Cayce, in describing the type of records the entity had studied during the Palestinian Period, said: "Those same records of which the men of the East said and gave, 'By those records we have seen His star.' These pertained, then, to what you would call today astrological forecasts, as well as those records which had been compiled and gathered by all of those of that period pertaining to the coming of the Messiah." Though Josephus mentions the Essene faculty for foretelling the future, he does not refer to astrology as the means, and this aspect of Essene life remained unknown.

Then the Qumran literature was discovered. Professor Burrows, in his excellent books on the scrolls, accredits Father Milik for the information "that a fragmentary document from Cave Four gives the signs of the zodiac and connects them with the months and days of each month; it also states the meaning of thunder under a particular sign." And Professor Allegro, in his equally excellent study, reports this:

"We have a number of their (Essenes) works referring to the movements of the heavenly bodies, and not all their study was of purely academic interest. For them the stars and their positions could affect men's lives, and amongst their esoteric documents we have one describing the influence of the heavenly bodies on the physical and spiritual characteristics of those born in certain sections of the Zodiac. One man will be hairy, or long-limbed, or stumpy-fingered, or, more important, be possessed of an abundance or otherwise of the Good Spirit, so that his whole being will be affected according to the sign of the Zodiac which he may claim for his own. And above all, they doubtless looked for a particular constellation which would tell them of a special birth, the coming of One for whom they and the whole Jewish world waited. We need not look far from Bethlehem to find a school of thought from which the Magi story of Matthew could have come."

Thus the scientists fill in more of the tapestry which may one day present the complete picture of Jesus and the Essenes precisely as Edgar Cayce described it.

At present, there is no way to evaluate scientifically the nature of Edgar Cayce's psychic faculties. Research into the psychic realm is being done at a number of important universities, and all that has been determined is that certain people do have the faculty of extrasensory perception, certain people do have the faculty of divination, certain people do have the faculty of possessing knowledge which they made no effort to acquire. That is all that has been established today. But as Father Teilhard proffered, man is progressing consistently, irresistibly, inescapably to the perfection of his world, losing ground only when he lets a lack of love and thought detour him to war, hate, violence, extremism and injustice. Each time man gets back on the track, he moves ahead. In light of this, in all likelihood the answer to all the psychic mysteries which surround us today is waiting just ahead to be discovered—or perhaps rediscovered after being stifled by cautiousness or lost by carelessness.

As things are, it would not be merely self-defensive to suggest that the Qumran experts wouldn't place much value on the information about the world of Jesus which was produced by the Edgar Cayce Readings. On the other hand, the world of Jesus may never be accurately known until it is established where a man like Cayce derived his authority to speak.

Edgar Cayce was convinced that his authority came from God.

And yet, in view of the lingering secrecy in Jerusalem, maybe this is already known.

THE A.R.E. TODAY

The Association for Research and Enlightenment, Inc., is a non-profit, open membership organization committed to spiritual growth, holistic healing, psychical research and its spiritual dimensions; and more specifically, to making practical use of the psychic readings of the late Edgar Cayce. Through nationwide programs, publications and study groups, A.R.E. offers all those interested, practical information and approaches for individual study and application to better understand and relate to themselves, to other people and to the universe. A.R.E. membership and outreach is concentrated in the United States with growing involvement throughout the world.

The headquarters at Virginia Beach, Virginia, include a library/conference center, administrative offices and publishing facilities, and are served by a beachfront motel. The library is one of the largest metaphysical, parapsychological libraries in the country. A.R.E. operates a bookstore, which also offers mail-order service and carries approximately 1,000 titles on nearly every subject related to spiritual growth, world religions, parapsychology and transpersonal psychology. A.R.E. serves its members through nationwide lecture programs, publications, a Braille library, a camp and an extensive Study Group Program.

The A.R.E. facilities, located at 67th Street and Atlantic Avenue, are open year-round. Visitors are always welcome and may write A.R.E., P.O. Box 595, Virginia Beach, VA 23451, for more information about the Association.